Praise for *Get Up*

"Every single person should own Bucky Sinister's 12-Step book. Addict or not. It is an incredibly funny and interesting guide on how to successfully unpack one's mind when it's over-packed. Simply put, this book should replace every magazine in every plastic surgeon's office and every bible in every motel."
—Amber Tamblyn, Emmy– and Golden Globe–nominated actress and poet

"This book is rad."
—Michelle Tea, author of *Rent Girl* and *Valencia*

"I have been sober for more than 21 years, and this is the first time I have seen anyone take on the challenges of staying with a 12-Step program with such frankness. This is one of the best recovery books I have read, a whole new approach written with intelligence and honesty. Bucky's way of addressing the Higher Power concept will serve to help the millions of people out there who struggle with it every day."
—Tom Callan, president of Board of Directors of Changing Echos, a drug and alcohol treatment center

"A must-have for the freakshow of life. . . . Sober-rific."
—Dannyboy S., tattoo installer

"Finally! Help getting clean from ONE OF US! The inimitable Bucky Sinister has won over audiences at readings in every bar in San Francisco for almost 20 years and now he has some sound advice for the newly sober on how to walk into them without a relapse."
—Eric Lyle, author of *On the Lower Frequencies, A Secret History of the City*

Also by Bucky Sinister

King of the Roadkills
Whiskey and Robots
All Blacked & Nowhere to Go

Comedy CD: *What Happens in Narnia, Stays in Narnia*

Chapbooks:
12 Bowls of Glass
Asphalt Rivers
A Friend and a Killer
Symphony of the Damned
NASCAR
Blackout Poems for Drunk Readers
Tragedy and Bourbon
Fever Dreams
Angels We Have Heard While High

Get Up

GET UP

A 12-STEP GUIDE TO RECOVERY FOR MISFITS, FREAKS & WEIRDOS

BUCKY SINISTER

First published in 2008 by Conari Press,
an imprint of Red Wheel/Weiser, LLC
With offices at:
500 Third Street, Suite 230
San Francisco, CA 94107
www.redwheelweiser.com

ISBN: 978-1-57324-366-7
Library of Congress Cataloging-in-Publication Data available upon request.

Cover Illustration and chapter titles © Chuck Sperry
Text design by Donna Linden
Typeset in Adobe Caslon and Impact
Cover photograph © Raina Bird

Printed in Canada
TCP
10 9 8 7 6 5 4 3 2 1

The paper used in this publication meets the minimum requirements of the
American National Standard for Information Sciences—Permanence of Paper
for Printed Library Materials Z39.48-1992 (R1997).

There were some people who were really important to my recovery who have since relapsed and are back in the throes of addiction. Of course, I'm not mentioning them by name. You know where I am, where you should be. It's time to come home.

This book is dedicated to the addict who still suffers.

CONTENTS

ACKNOWLEDGMENTS

The information in this book was gathered in my mind after many late night milkshakes, over the pain of tattoo ink applied to me, from rides home after meetings, and over-caffeinated ramblings of the recovering minds. It's late night phone calls, desperate instant messages, and overtyped emails. There's no one person who helped me more than the others, from MFA holders to ex-cons on parole. CEOs and reformed gangbangers alike have contributed to the mishmash of knowledge I now share with you.

Thanks to Maggie for putting up with me during the entire process of this book, listening to my thoughts, reading my work, and giving me a sounding board for every idea in here.

Thanks most of all to Amber, my editor, for convincing me to write the book in the first place. There should be many more freakout anxiety calls coming your way; thanks for always talking me down.

INTRODUCTION

What This Book Is

This is a recovery book written by a guy who never thought he'd read one all the way through. I never liked any of the self-help or spirituality books I saw. I thought they were trite, or pandered to the perpetually wounded soul. Many of them recycled the same self-affirmations that were in other books. Frankly, a lot of them I thought were total bullshit.

I'm a strict atheist. I'm a cynic. I'm a freak, a weirdo, a misfit. I've spent as much time growing up in fundamentalist circles as I did in the punk scene. I'm also an alcoholic and drug addict who hasn't picked up a drink or a drug since 2002. I went into 12-Step recovery with as much reluctance as I could muster while still giving it a try. Now I love the program's steps and traditions, and I look forward to the meeting I run every week and the ones I go to for fun.

You read that right . . . for *fun*. Yes, the meetings are fun. They are as fun as a revival or a really good punk show. My favorite aspects of going out to bars—namely the camaraderie, the BS sessions, and the new people to meet—are all much better at meetings. Some of my friends ask me if I still go to meetings after all this time sober, and it stuns me that they don't realize that I *like* to go. But it wasn't always fun for me.

I knew I had to quit drinking, but I didn't want to go to meetings. What I wanted was to go to some really nice celebrity rehab center, the kind where Ben Affleck or Danny Bonaduce gets to go, where I could sit around in a thick bathrobe and Ray-Bans while networking my next book-to-movie deal with my feet in the pool. That didn't work out. I had negative money, no health insurance, and no chance at getting in any place like that. 12-Step meetings were my only option, but I was still reluctant.

The 12-Step groups are free. There are no dues or fees. People will pick you up and give you a ride if that's an issue. I didn't want to go, but I couldn't beat the price, and it was imperative that I did something.

The last place I wanted to be was in a church basement. I've been in more church basements than shitty green paint. I've eaten many lifetimes' worth of tuna casserole and Frito pie at potlucks in these basements. But I'll be damned if that isn't where most 12-Step meetings are.

The meetings being my only option, I had to suck it up and go. My way had damn near killed me. I needed other ideas, outside help, and the only people who would do it for free were a bunch of people who had been in my same situation.

I struggled with each aspect of the program. For a long time, I just practiced Step 1 over and over. That's the step where you decide to not drink or use anymore, because it's fucking up your life. My first meeting, I wasn't sure that I was powerless over alcohol, but I knew without a doubt that my life was unmanageable, like it says in Step 1. Still, I struggled, keeping my own pace.

The last place I wanted to be was in a church basement. I've been in more church basements than shitty green paint.

It took me longer to get through the steps than anyone else I've met who hasn't relapsed. I stayed on a step for months or years if necessary. I didn't even say the full Serenity Prayer for the first three years I was in, because it had the word *God* at the beginning of it. It was like there were two of me, one dragging the other one through the program.

But I've come full circle, and I want to share my thoughts and experiences with other people who are suspicious of 12 Steppers and their coffee-chugging meetings. It's okay to think they all look a little desperate and weird, chain-smoking like that outside the back door of a church building at 6 P.M. on a Friday night. It's okay to wonder if these people really mean it when they say you can call them "anytime" when you just met them a minute ago. It's okay to be cynical, skeptical, and a little freaked out by the whole situation. That's what this book is about, really. It's encouragement to give something that looks ridiculous a shot at saving your life.

What It's Not

This is not a book that will solve your problems. You will have to do that yourself. Whether your problems were caused by forces outside your control or were self-inflicted, you're the only one who has the ability to overcome your own struggles. This book will encourage you to find the proper help for your problems.

This is not a book against 12-Step programs. Think of 12 Step as a set of tools, and you have to build a house. You're building that house on your own, and you'll have to live in it when you're done. The advice I give will help you learn how to use those tools to build the house that best suits you.

This is not a book that will lead to you buying DVDs, going to seminars, or taking workshops. I've seen a lot of other people with a This-Is-The-Answer book that is nothing more than a text version of an infomercial for what they're really selling. I'm trying to encourage you to seek help from an established community near you, one that won't charge you a dime for their services.

This is not a book that will ask you to believe in any spiritual dogmatic system, any religion, or subscribe to any established philosophical trope. I'm not mishmashing Eastern religions; I'm not rehashing self-help gurus from years past; and I'm not slamming a view of life, the universe, and everything down your throat. I'm also not telling you that whatever religion or philosophy you have is the wrong one. I do want to clear out some of the clutter in your mind so you're free to think about who you really are and get a clear picture of what you believe.

> **This is not a book that will ask you to believe in any spiritual dogmatic system, any religion, or subscribe to any established philosophical trope.**

I want you to read this book with an open mind. If you're anything like me, you're looking for the first thing you disagree with that you will use to discount the entire book.

I'm not perfect, consistent, or absolute. I'm a hardheaded addict with a few ideas that you could use for yourself. I'm not trying to save you. I want you to save yourself.

Chapter 1

12 Step for the Rest of Us

I'm not sure why you're reading this book right now. Maybe someone who loves you and is concerned for you gave you this book. Maybe you picked it up because you're worried about yourself. Maybe you're already searching through 12-Step communities but feel like your needs aren't being addressed. Maybe you've been in a 12-Step program but don't like any of the literature. Whatever it may be, my goal is to help you move past your problems into the next phase of your life.

What I'm going to assume is that you don't fit in well with others. Maybe this is true; maybe it's how you feel about yourself. Regardless of the truth of the matter, you're not comfortable with the status quo. You're wary of being one of the herd. If everyone goes in one door, you want to go out the window. If everyone jumps off a cliff, you jump off a bridge. What I'm saying is, you may not be making the right decisions, but at least you're not making the same wrong decisions that everyone else is making. From this perspective, 12-Step programs are a scary place.

> **What I'm going to assume is that you don't fit in well with others.**

At the beginning, everyone mumbles out the same prayer from memory. That's an auspicious start to any group meeting. You don't like prayers, you don't like group chantings. *Everyone's sharing a brain,* you think. *This is the Borg. Is it some kind of weird cult?* Then it gets worse.

Somebody says a name. Everyone, in unison, greets that person with the same greeting. That person talks, and tells some horrible story, during which the rest of the group laughs. *What the fuck? What is so fucking funny?* Then it gets worse.

How much coffee can these people drink? Halfway through this meeting, a good portion of the room got up to go outside and smoke, and they were smoking right before it started; isn't that an addiction too? Then it gets worse.

The guy who drives my shuttle bus every day just told the room that he's a horrible crack addict. He has six months clean . . . that means he was all cracked out driving me to work every day for years. Over there is the cranky guy from the corner deli. Is that my ex sitting in the front row? Dude, there are at least three bartenders in here right now.

All of this inner dialogue is normal. 12 Step is a little freaky at first. You'll see all kinds of people from your life, both dear friends and people you recognize from the neighborhood but don't really know. What you're going to have to get over is your preconception that these people have nothing to offer you, that they have nothing in common with you.

I've been around many different subcultures since the '80s. Punks, skinheads, Goths, skaters, rockabillies, Wiccans, vegans, slam poets, comedians, break-dancers, bikers, hip-hop thugs, gangstas both real and self-imagined. Inside each of these subcultures are even smaller subcultures: anarchists, animal rights activists, tech geeks, graffiti artists. I've been close by many of these groups but never felt like I was fully a part of any of them.

When it comes down to it, I'm a loner. Lonerism is a self-

> I've been around many different subcultures since the '80s ... but never felt like I was fully a part of any of them.

inflicted lifestyle. I isolate from others. If I find out that I'm fitting into a group, I find reasons that I don't fit so I can feel left out. I use my skepticism and cynicism to distance myself from the group mentality. It's saved me from joining gangs, mobs, and groups that would not be good for me; it has also kept me from developing the close relationships that I needed to grow as a person. No matter whether the group accepts me or not, I don't accept that I'm a part of it.

People who can readily accept being part of a group will take to 12-Step recovery much faster. Those who don't question the immediate help and friendship offered by the group will embrace the overwhelmingly positive parts of the program. It's a secure feeling to them that there are rooms full of people willing to help in nearly every capacity. But for you, You-Who-Do-Not-Fit-In, it's going to take some work. This book is for you.

Three Types of People

For our purposes, there are three types of people out there: Normies, Addicts, and Recovering Addicts. Normies are the normal people, who drink now and then and maybe tried drugs, but for some reason, they don't get addicted or overindulge. Addicts are people for whom drug and alcohol use supersede personal will. Recovering Addicts are addicts who no longer use and work to remove the obsession to use. This book is written for all three types, but mainly for someone who wants to move from the second group into the third.

Nature Versus Nurture

Why do some people get addicted and others don't? Is it genetic? Or is it a product of one's immediate culture? Are you born an addict or made into one? From a purely observational point of view, I think it's a combination of both. The only reason it matters is so that you see you shouldn't take an extended break from using or try to cut back. You have a lifetime of stimuli and a physiology that makes drinking and drug use entirely dangerous.

My point of view is this: You may start a Normie, but once you become an Addict, you can't go back to being a Normie, and once you become a Recovering Addict, you can't go back to being an Addict. People will fight me on the last part of this when they read it, but stay with me, I'll explain. This movement across definitions is an evolution of character. Once you make the successful transformation, you don't go back.

I started a Normie. I didn't touch a thing until I was seventeen. I didn't drink, smoke pot, or even smoke cigarettes until then. I drank when I had easy access to it and when it would not jeopardize my situation. I didn't go out of my way to find it, nor did I use it if I thought it wasn't prudent at the time. But when I did drink, I drank to get as fucked up as possible. That was a bad habit that led me to being an addict.

I come from a line of alcoholics, like many alcoholics do. On the nature side of things, I know that there was a history in my family. On the nurture side of things, while my father never drank, he was raised by a drunk, and therefore acted like one all the time, what we call a "dry drunk." It's the way he learned how to deal with other people.

There were always a lot of people in my house. I have two sisters. There were usually cousins or a student of my father's living with us. During the summers, my mother's sister would come with her kids and stay with us. There were various members of my dad's church who came for indeterminate amounts of time. I bring this up because of our food situation and my lack of control around consumption.

There was always enough food for us, but never too much. If we had a box of cereal, the most I could get at was a bowl and a half. At dinner, there might be seconds of one dish or another, but not much more than that. If there was pie at dessert, we each got a tiny piece and then it was gone. I never went hungry as a child, but I never had to learn when to say no to food either. There were a couple of instances when this didn't happen, and they stick out in my mind.

Occasionally, my sisters would go off to church camp, and I'd be left alone like an only child, which seemed the grandest luxury in the world. Not only did I have my choice of television shows, but my choice of seat while watching the show. I could have friends over without us being terrorized by my older sisters and their friends. Best of all, I got to choose the restaurant we went to for lunch after church.

One such weekend, my sisters were gone, my dad was out of town, and there were no other people in tow. It was just my mother and I. She told me we could go wherever we wanted to go. It was either Bonanza or Sizzler, I don't remember which, but I remember the meal well. I got the steak with the all-you-can-eat shrimp. I ate the steak, and started in on the shrimp. I finished the shrimp and asked for more. The waitress brought me more and made some remark about that should do me. I was going to show her. I finished that plate and asked her for thirds. She made a big deal about me being able to eat a lot, which was probably an insult in her mind, but I thought it was great.

My mom was of the generation where a kid who eats a lot is healthy and growing. Besides that, anything that wasn't expressly candy or dessert was good for you, whether it was battered, fried, or whatever cut of meat—it didn't matter. Whatever Bisquick casserole she made I ate with reckless abandon. I routinely had eggs, bacon (what we called "fatback"), and pancakes for breakfast. Lunch was sandwiches grilled in butter, or hot dogs. Dinner was more ordinary *Good Housekeeping* kind of fare, but the side dishes were carb heavy and often a colored gooey Cool Whip mess she called Ambrosia. I think the only thing that saved me from a junior high heart attack was that a lot of the meat I ate at dinner was very lean wild game that my father killed in the fall and that we ate from the deep freeze all year-round. My point is that my mom was the last lady in the town who was going to tell me not to have thirds, or fourths, even, although she'd be strict with dessert.

I'm not sure how much I had, but finally I was coaxed into leaving. I remember the heat coming through the window of the station wagon warming my neck. It reminded me of the time at the county fair when I was convinced to get on the Tilt-A-Whirl. *Oh no,* I thought, *I'm going to barf.*

Barf I did. All that batter-fried shrimp was returned to the sea from which it came. I had never been sick from eating before. The good news is I got to stay home from school on Monday.

This was the only time I didn't go back to what made me ill, but there were many other instances of excess. As I got older and the house emptied out of people, I'd eat a box of cereal after school, from ripping open the lining to the golden powder pouring in the bowl. After two bowls, my gums were torn up and hurting, but I wouldn't stop until the bowl was empty. After it was gone, I'd try to eat dinner a few hours later with my gums cut and my tongue rubbed raw. The next week the same brand of cereal would be there, and I'd do it again. The only thing that stopped me when I started eating was running out.

I drank exactly the same way from the time I started. I never left a beer or a cocktail unfinished. I'd buy half-pints of vodka or whiskey in my younger days and drink the whole thing. That seemed to be enough for me until I started buying pints; then a pint of whiskey was what I had to drink before I passed out. The fifth bottle proved my nemesis for many years, as I would drink most of it before passing out. But soon enough, I found myself finishing those over three or four hours while watching TV. Somewhere around that time I'd find my way back to the liquor store completely wasted, but still wanting more. There were nights when I couldn't stand up, but as I lay on the floor looking at the empty whiskey bottle on the coffee table, I'd think about how I wished I had another bottle.

So is it a matter of my nature that I couldn't control my eating as a child, and therefore couldn't control my drinking as an adult? Or is it a matter of nurture that I was allowed to eat as much as I did, and was never taught self-control? Is self-control something that can be taught to another individual, or is it something we learn through trial and error? If we learn it ourselves, are there those of us who are incapable of learning it? I don't know the answers to these questions. But what I do know is clear: I have self-control issues when it comes to physical things that give me pleasure.

Often people will offer me a bite of ice cream or a bit of their chocolate whatever. I usually decline. They usually force it on me. If I have one bite, when we part ways, I'm at the corner store buying a pint of Ben & Jerry's and thinking about what pint I will buy the next day. I'm obsessive about ingesting food. The bad side is, this food is bad for my health. The good side is, if I eat a pint of ice cream, I don't call my ex-girlfriends at 2 A.M.

When I drank whiskey this way, I combined a self-control problem with a substance that is physically addictive and lowers inhibition. There is no set of circumstances in which this turns out well. There are no tools left to fight the compulsion to drink more. The only things that would stop me at this point are the liquor store closing, running out of money, or getting thrown out of the bar after last call.

Where Everybody Doesn't Know Your Name

On 16th Street in San Francisco there's a bar called The Kilowatt. This is where I drank on Sunday mornings with The Boys. We watched football and drank like men. Andy, the bartender, made me bourbon and Cokes in pint glasses. From 10 A.M. to 4 P.M. we watched the brutal ballet that is the National Football League. Outside, Rob grilled the meat, and we were all bonding.

Many were the Sunday afternoons when I'd bid farewell to The Boys and stagger off to the BART station to make my way home, to catch HBO's Sunday night lineup with a nightcap of bourbon. All in all, a good day indeed, spent drinking well over a quart of whiskey.

I thought that if I quit drinking I'd let everyone down. They'd miss me. The bar wouldn't be the same without One of the Boys, would it? I was the literary one of the bar. I imagined myself to be the Frasier of the 16th Street Cheers. I was the hard-drinking, underappreciated-in-his-own-time writer, whose published book had unfortunately been ahead of its time.

There was no way I could let them see me in the bar during football without a drink. It would be much like seeing Barry Bonds limp after a pop fly in his later years, or watching a boxer past his prime step into the ring, or listening to the Aerosmith album they did right after they quit doing cocaine. It wouldn't be right. Luckily for me, I got sober in February, as the Super Bowl was wrapping up the NFL postseason.

I approached the bartender, Andy.

"I'm thinking about getting sober," I admitted.

"That's a great idea," he said without hesitation. When your bartender really wants you to quit, it's time.

Further than that, if you don't know who the worst drunk is in your favorite bar, it's you. When you quit, someone else becomes the worst drunk in the bar. They've all been comparing themselves to you, saying, "At least I'm not that guy." Quitting is threatening to them. Your drinking validates their drinking. You may know a lot of people who drink as much as you do; you also know a lot of other alcoholics.

For you drug types out there, if you don't know someone who hasn't tried cocaine, you're an addict. You've surrounded yourself with a social circle that thinks it's normal to do cocaine, even if it's a now-and-then situation. Most people in this country will never try cocaine or heroin. Most of them will never even have the opportunity. You've created this world for yourself with a reality to which you shouldn't compare yourself.

Drinking during the day, drinking whiskey in the morning didn't seem odd to me, since I knew plenty of other people who did it. Most people I knew did it, because I had created a world of problem drinkers around me. The people I knew drank every single day after work in the same bars.

That fall, I returned to The Kilowatt with about half a year sober. Andy poured me a root beer, and I handed him some poems I'd written since he'd seen me last.

"What are you reading," one of The Boys asked.

"Some of Bucky's new shit," Andy told him.

"Who's Bucky?"

"This guy," Andy said.

He looked right at me. No recognition whatsoever.

"Nice to meet you," he said.

It hit me. He didn't know me. I looked around the bar at the rest of The Boys. There was Panama Hat, Guy Who Drinks Corona With Lime, Redskins Fan With Ponytail . . . I didn't know these guys. They didn't know me. They weren't my friends at all. They were random jerks at the bar. And I was a more random jerk from off the street.

So Life You in the Nads

First off, apologies for the decidedly male metaphor here. *Gut Punch* would work as well, but it doesn't quite have the same ring to it. The days of the Gut Punch are long over, anyway; few people have been randomly socked in the midsection, but guys all around the world still know what a good racking will do.

Anyone who has partaken in playground violence understands the equalizer that is the Kick in the Nads. No matter how tough that bully is, anyone else can take him down with one well-placed Buster Brown.

In adult life, there are events that are unforeseen and shattering to the psyche. Usually it's the death of a loved one or a child, but it can also be finan-

cial disaster or any number of things. The event is so traumatic that it renders the eventee helpless and incapable of dealing with the rest of life. This is when a lot of people cross the line from having had a drink or a drug to becoming full-blown addicts.

Many addicts grew their dependence over a lifetime of poor emotional and social choices. The Nad Kick takes people who were otherwise successful in life and reduces them quickly. The Kickee's social group enables the bad behavior, since he or she seems to deserve to get drunk or high. No one blames him for a bender or prolonged depression. But the danger with dealing with a Nad Kick by using drugs and alcohol is that the depression sometimes sticks.

Ever have someone tell you, "Don't make a face like that, it might stay that way?" Or were you told that if someone slapped you on the back while you made a nasty face it would stick? Consider your depression the nasty face and a drug bender that slap on the back.

The physical part of your addiction will make an alliance with your misery; as long as it's okay for you to drink when you're miserable, then the part of you that wants the vice will keep you miserable so you keep self-medicating. Before too long, your physical addiction will be strongly tied into a dark emotional state.

It's hard for the Kickees in 12 Step. Most of the Steppers can't point to a specific incident to relate to why they started drinking. The Kickee can. The easy thing to feel is an addict's superiority complex. The others don't seem to have a real reason to be drinking; they seem to have been born addicts. The only bad things that ever happened to them were of their own design. Life for the Kickee was going great until The Event.

Clean and Sober Versus Straight Edge

When I first found the punk scene in the '80s, I felt like I was home. I had come out of a crazy religious upbringing that was either extreme fundamentalism or a mind-controlling cult. Neither part of my childhood appealed to me anymore. When I got around punks for the first time, I was relieved to find that there was a group of people who also hated society and couldn't accept what it had done to us.

I believed the government and organized religion were oppressing us. They worked hand in hand to deny us of our right to make our own moral choices about gay rights, abortion, and snorting coke. While cigarettes and alcohol were perfectly legal, marijuana wasn't, and you can make pants and paper out of marijuana. To show my protest against such abusive powers, I drank as much hard liquor as I could get my underage hands on.

But no party is complete without its poopers, and for me, those were the Straight Edge kids. The Straight Edge scene started as a response to Minor Threat songs, in which Ian MacKaye sang about not getting high, drunk, or screwing. I loved Minor Threat, but there was no way I was abstaining from drugs or alcohol. I was abstaining from sex, but that wasn't my choice—that was the cruel choice of awkward teenage pubescence. I was trying really hard not to abstain from that one. The Straight Edgers were obnoxious fucks who looked like skinheads and acted like militant Mormons.

Straight Edgers were notorious for ruining the good times of others. The classic move was when they'd knock the beer out of someone's hand at a show. Other more subtle moves would be when they'd ask for a hit off your contraband vodka half-pint, and then drop it on the floor on purpose. The most obnoxious move was the SE Cockblock. When you were getting up to talk to the unbearably cute punk girl, and were passing her your drink, they'd stand around and scowl. They were hard to fight, since they traveled in packs and they were completely sober.

Out of all the multitude of factions of the punk scene, there were those who drank and those who did not. The ones who drank were clearly the ones having the most fun. I went to parties in Oakland with all strata of punks and got entirely wasted. There was one legendary party for me in which my friend K___ got a 5-foot tank of nitrous oxide and her whole house sat around with the huge balloons, getting ripped all night. The kids who didn't drink or get high? I didn't know where they were that night, but they definitely were missing out.

But when I was sober, I never felt like I fit in. Looking back on it now, I'm sure that was the addict in me knowing I would drink or use anything as long as everyone else was doing it, and it would make me feel like one of the group. The

> **I had no idea that everyone at every party I went to wasn't getting as wasted as I was.**

East Bay Punx have their own styles of living, talking, and dressing. They have their own music, stories, and recreation. I never felt like I knew enough of them, no matter how many of them I met. I always felt like the new guy, even after more than ten years on the scene. There was a small circle of them who had broken down my wall, and I was afraid I wouldn't have them in my life if I wasn't drinking with them.

I didn't want to get sober and have to hang out with the Straight Edgers. Although by the time I was thirty-one, I didn't know many SEs anymore. Many of them didn't stay militant SE for their whole lives; they either started drinking at twenty-one or stopped giving everyone else a hard time about it. What I didn't realize is that there were plenty of Clean and Sober and Never Drank punks out there.

I had no idea that everyone at every party I went to wasn't getting as wasted as I was. I really believed that everyone else pounded back shots and beer to get to blackout heaven, and did drugs like cocaine to help them drink longer. There were people around me the entire time who either had never had a drink or had quit for good.

Even now, I sometimes have people come up to me and tell me how wasted I was at a party the weekend before. I have to tell them, no, I haven't had a drink since 2002. They swear to me that I was doing all kinds of shit, drunk off my ass. Either they have the wrong person, or they were projecting their own inebriation just like I used to do.

It took me more than a month after quitting drinking to get into a 12-Step meeting. A former bartender, who used to give me rides home from the bar because she didn't trust me to get home in a cab, called me up and offered me a ride. I had no idea she wasn't a drinker. I thought I'd go to a meeting to humor her, and then tell her it wasn't for me. But when I got there, I liked it. I enjoyed the story the speaker told. I thought it would be easy to go and sit in the back of these things and drink coffee.

But after a few meetings, it was really getting to me. I was still less than broke, and though I wasn't drinking, I wasn't having any fun either. I looked around at everyone, and they seemed different. One guy talked about living in his car during his bottom; I thought he was pretty lucky to have a car. Another man talked about hiding his drinking from his wife and children; a man with a family who would stand with him through all this was truly fortunate. I was the outsider again, until I ran into an old friend of mine who was a few weeks sober.

"F___," I said, "what are you doing here?"

"Hey," he told me, "I got sober a couple of weeks ago. How are you doing?"

"I'm okay, but these people are driving me nuts."

"You gotta come with me to BNO."

"What's that?" I asked.

"It's a men's meeting on Valencia on Tuesdays. You'll like it."

I looked up the meeting on my schedule. Boys' Night Out. Sounded like a scout meeting or a bunch of gay men going shopping. But I trusted F___, and gave it a shot.

Outside the meeting, it looked like bands were about to play. There were punks, skins, and rockabilly guys of all sizes, shapes, and colors. They were all chain-smoking and hitting each other.

Running the meeting was a celebrity musician guy. He was in one of the bands that had broken through to the mainstream and had been played extensively on MTV. I didn't know what to think. Didn't he have his shit together? Why was he going to meetings? I read in *SPIN* or some shit that the whole band had gotten sober in the '90s. I figured he must have relapsed or something. Later I found out he had eight or nine years, which seemed like forever to me. I had no idea why anyone who had more than a year sober would go to a meeting.

When the meeting started, all hell broke loose. They opened with "a moment of violence followed by the Serenity Prayer," in which they all turned to a neighboring stooge and punched the crap out of his arm. They relentlessly heckled the guys who read the steps and traditions. They made Yo Momma jokes during peoples' shares. This is what F___ had in mind? These scumbags were going to save my life? They couldn't even shoot dope right, according to their own stories. How were they going to help me? Depression overwhelmed me.

Who are these happy arm-punching motherfuckers? What's so funny? I am trying to get sober, and they're cutting up and acting like they're in some dumbass locker room. If they had towels, they'd be snapping each others' asses by now. How the hell am I supposed to get sober? At least they're not the weird meditation and God people from the other meetings, I thought.

As an alcoholic, I didn't spend precious money paying cover charges for bands. I stayed home and drank whiskey with the money. The drinks in the clubs and bars were way overpriced. I often got way too wasted at the clubs anyway, and had to spend more money on cabs to get home.

As a freshly sober guy trying to remember what he did for fun, I started going to clubs again to watch bands. It was like going back to my old hometown: I remembered the way but couldn't remember the name of streets. I got to the club and paid my way in on instinct. It had been a long time.

Not getting a whiskey right away was unnatural. Was everyone staring at me? Could they all tell I was stone-cold sober? Would the bartenders be mad if I didn't drink? Out of place, out of sync, out of step. Once again, I didn't fit in, and the whiskey urged me to make it go away.

Off to the side of the regular crowd stood a handful of guys from BNO. I had never been so happy to see anyone from a meeting. I walked up to them. They stared blankly at me, sizing me up.

"I was at BNO on Tuesday," I yelled into a guy's ear.

"How much time you got?" he yelled back.

"Six weeks."

"First six months are the hardest," he said. "Keep coming back."

Somewhere in all that mess of fast music and BO I figured it out. These weren't Straight Edgers; these were Clean and Sober Punx. I'd jumped myself into a gang by abusing drugs and alcohol for fifteen years. I gave up my Loner colors, and let myself stand with others.

Get the Fuck Up

We've been there and come back. When you fall in the pit, people are supposed to help you up. But you have to get up on your own. We'll take your arms, but you'll have to get your legs underneath you and stand again.

My advice to you is simple: Get up. You're not going to get any better lying there like that.

My advice to you is simple: Get up. You're not going to get any better lying there like that. I know, it hurts, but you have to get up and walk it off. Get up. No one is going to help you. Get up. You have a whole life to live. Right now, you're stuck in the quicksand of self-pity, and you're asking for a rope of acknowledgment. I know it's my metaphor, but that rope isn't going to hold. That self-pity is going to destroy any chance you have at happiness, and it will eventually spiral out and destroy your relationships and your social life.

Finding a Sponsor

This may be your most difficult task if you are an atheist in a 12-Step program. Many sponsors won't put up with your atheist lifestyle; they'll likely read you a part of the Big Book, which, on the surface, seems to condemn atheism. If you read it more closely, it suggests that the road to recovery for an atheist will be more difficult.

Really, though, get a sponsor. Remember that your sponsor is only there to help you work the steps. He or she is not your best friend, your coach, your employment agent, or your therapist. Your sponsor is an equal to you. But your sponsor should be someone who's seen the program work a lot of different ways and has been through all the steps a number of times. The steps are trickier than they look initially; in fact, they're pretty vague.

Your sponsor shouldn't worry about your version of the Higher Power concept. He's not there to debate the cosmic structure with you or tell you to go to church. If your sponsor decides that he's going to give you advice about anything other than working the steps, maybe you should get another one. But be nice about it. He's only trying to help. Conversely, don't expect too much from your sponsor. Your sponsor is there for you, but it's you who has to do the actual work. This is like the rest of your recovery, as you have to take responsibility for your own actions. It's up to you to get your step work done.

Creating a Community

The 12-Step community relies upon stories for the core of its communication. They may call them "shares," but it's the same thing. The have a beginning, middle, and end, usually with a message. Sometimes it's a long meandering methadone ramble, but usually there's a point.

Feasibly, you can work steps on your own. It's good to have the initiative to do things at your own pace. But to gain the recovery that 12 Step offers, you really need to participate in a community. This is why I strongly discourage people who want to quit using without getting involved in a program. Users usually carry a lot of pain and misery that they don't need. Isolation makes the heart grow somber. Misery loves company, especially company more miserable than itself.

The Big Book Is Just a Rule Book

Monopoly and Risk were the two best ways to spend a preteen Friday night before Nintendo invented Tecmo Bowl and killed the board game industry. There were video games before that, but the best the Atari 2600 and the Intellivision had to offer couldn't compete with the geniuses at Parker Brothers and Milton Bradley. Families everywhere had board games. But while all the games inspired long readings from the rule books as to the exact interpretations of said rules, Monopoly's rules were meant to be broken, amended, and ignored.

No two families played Monopoly the same way. According to the rule book, the Free Parking space gets you no money, when a property is landed on but not purchased it goes up for auction, and when you run out of the toy houses or hotels, that's it, you're not allowed to substitute anything for them. But these three rules seem foreign even to veteran players. The rule book seemed like vague guidelines for play.

That's the way I see recovery meetings. All of them are a little different, but they're all using the same book. Some allow no drug talk, others do. There are speaker meetings, speaker/discussion meetings, Big Book readings, and step studies. There are different types of people in each one, varying in gender, ethnicity, social class, and age. Emphasis on Higher Powers vary from meeting to meeting. If there's something that irritates you about one meeting, try another.

There are as many different types of meetings as there are bars. Just as there are many bars you would never ever go to, there are likely meetings that you will never like either. But just like your favorite bars, if you look long enough, you will find a meeting that feels like home. Once you feel that community of the meetings, you won't miss the bars so much.

My favorite part of the poetry readings I went to back in the '90s were what happened afterward. It was the best place to look if I was looking for trouble to get into later. I loved rolling into some bar with a bunch of crazy poets and tearing the place up. As morose and defeatist as many of them were in their writing, they were lots of fun when they had a few drinks in them. Getting wasted and talking about writing, bad readings we'd had, and gossiping about other writers was a blast.

The meetings have a similar dynamic. Now I get the same feeling as before when a dozen of us all meet up at some restaurant. It's great to walk into a place, say that we have twelve coming, then count them as the motorcycles pull up on the sidewalk and cars pull up with a number of riders spilling out clown-like from the seats.

What Do You Want, a Cookie?

Little victories are the ones you'll celebrate in your first few months of sobriety. You'll pay your phone bill on time. You won't have $300 ATM withdrawals that you don't remember. You'll get to work every day. But no one in the rest of the world will care. You can tell them, "Hey! I've gone a whole week without blacking out!" and they will not understand what a big deal that is. Perhaps someone will say, "What do you want, a cookie?"

In 12 Step, we often *have* cookies for you, in the back near the coffee. I know that's a cheap metaphor, but it works here. You can stick up your hand and share any of your successes and get legitimate applause. You can also tell other people that you are thirty-three years old and don't know how to work a washing machine, and no one will really question it. They'll help you.

The stories told in the meetings are going to do you more good than any other passive activity in 12 Step. All you have to do is sit and listen. The steps require action, but the stories require your presence and attention. At many meetings, you will be able to sit there with a cup of coffee and a handful of cookies. How much better do you want your life? You haven't been treated this well since kindergarten. Cookies, coffee, and the story of The Little Junkie That Could. The only thing better would be if it came with a nap.

We're here for dumb questions and the victories too dumb to share with the rest of the world. If you can turn a tape recorder into a tattoo gun, but don't know how to use a checkbook, you're in the right place. If you can broker a coke deal between two parties, neither of whom speaks the same language you do, but you don't know how to go on a job interview, you're in the right place. If you know how to steal cable, but don't know how to get it legitimately, you're in the right place. Just ask. We'll help. We may laugh a little, but only because we've been there.

Chapter 2

The God Problem

The number one hesitation I hear from people thinking of joining a 12-Step group is they're scared of the Higher Power concept. Getting right to the point, I'm a strict atheist, and I have no problems with the Higher Power. If the Higher Power concept, or as I thought of it in my early days, The God Problem, is what is keeping you from 12-Step recovery, go ahead and join a group. You have no excuse.

My Background in Religion

I grew up a preacher's kid in a fundamentalist Christian family. I was taught to memorize scripture before I could read. My father was on the road preaching forty weekends out of every year, as what most people would call an evangelist, but we simply called a preacher. As far back as I remember, I always wanted to be a preacher myself.

Like other kids idolized athletes or rock stars, I idolized preachers. I lived in a neighborhood that housed the faculty of the local Christian university, and I had men of God living all around me. Every morning as I watched my father walk out of the house and to his work, I saw the other men in their cheap suits and unmovable hair walk to the nearby campus. I saw them in the woods when my father took me hunting, and I saw them in the boats when we went fishing. But best of all, I saw them in the pulpits at church.

I loved the way they commanded attention, how they sweated through the cheap JCPenney suits, the way they held the microphone like a pair of brass knuckles, the colors their faces turned, the veins that stuck out in their heads, and the angry timbre in their voices that were worn low and smooth from years of hellfire and brimstone. There was something innately cool about it, even as a young boy, that was as cool as watching a demolition derby or jumping ramps with a dirt bike: I couldn't wait for it to be my turn. Ahead of me was high school, then a Bible college, and the small starter gigs that young preachers can get. Eventually I wanted to get my PhD like my father had, along with his master's degrees. With their recommendation and my genes, there was nothing to stop me from getting what I wanted.

At the age of thirteen, the dream began to unravel. My father uncovered an interweaving series of embezzlement, misappropriation of funds, fraud, and illegal scholarships that were rampant in the university where he taught, and had been perpetrated by men that I looked up to. These men were not only university faculty, but their other roles were leadership positions in our church. Money, power, and prestige were more important to these men than their ethics. I didn't know what place I would have as an adult with these men.

There were a group of churches that had split away from our brotherhood for various issues. They were more evangelical, ran street ministries, and kept much closer tabs on each other than I'd ever experienced before. Better than all that, they wanted my family when the rest of the churches were turning their backs on us.

We moved to the new church in 1984. I spent the next three years inviting more than a thousand people to study the Bible with me. I took beatings on the street from gang members and thugs who didn't like me being out there, or were just sadistic and loved the chaos and pain they inflicted. I fought with members of the Unification Church, the Nation of Islam, and various other groups for good recruiting territory. Within a year, I was deeply involved in the church's street ministry. But things went too far there as well.

I can't express the levels of deceit and dishonesty I found in this new church. We were told to pretend to like people in order to get them to join our church. We deliberately never told them what would be expected of them once they were in. We extracted secrets from people only to emotionally blackmail them later. I knew something was wrong. I was too young to even think about what they were doing with money; we took in enormous sums on a weekly basis, but there never was enough.

Years later, this church appeared in many books and on many TV shows about cults. Accusing them with this label or naming them would start a fight I don't want to participate in. I only write of this here so you understand the religious trauma I've experienced.

So I went back to the fundamentalist church of my youth. I had no idea where else to turn. The way I saw it, by the time I worked my way to a position of power, my father's old enemies would be long out of their positions.

One Sunday night, while in the pulpit of some hick church in the middle of Arkansas, I had the realization that religion was all bullshit. It was all a game. What had sounded so real coming out of my mouth in the past now sounded like some crazy story I was making up. I didn't believe any of it from that moment. I had conned people well because I believed my own scam. All my life, I'd been taught that the smoke and mirrors were tools to show everyone that the illusion was real.

The next Friday, I was in a trailer park getting drunk on four and a half cans of Old Milwaukee 1851. The weekend after that, I had the most delicious drink handed to me. I asked what it was. Whiskey and Coke, I was told. I went to other things in my life, but the whiskey and Coke was the standard to which I always returned.

Over the next few years I was still open to other religions, but I could never trust that they were honest at the core. Ideas may be pure, but the hearts of people are susceptible to temptation. I searched for a while, declared myself agnostic for a time, then came to accept that I was an atheist.

Why 12 Step, If I Don't Believe in All the Higher Power Crap?

Community, or the lack thereof, is the sickest part of American society. It's not the government that's the problem, although that's close behind. It's not about our health care, or even our still-imposed-upon civil rights, although those need attention as well. Because of our technology, geography, and class system, we're losing our sense of community.

A person can go for days without really sharing an important emotion with another human being. We don't know our neighbors. We listen to iPods more than to other people. No one talks on the bus, the elevator, or in line. We have our work friends but we exchange nothing more than congenialities and minor personal trivia. We spend an hour getting ready for work, and an hour getting to work, eight or more hours at work, and an hour coming home five days a week. The few hours each weeknight are commonly spent with nonpersonal distractions such as television or online

Even if you can afford other amenities, you need a community at your back.

gaming. Some people have families, but they don't really have much time to spend with them on a quality level. We see each other coming and going but rarely get to do anything together. This is why families have pizza night, why grown men join softball leagues, and gamers get together in the flesh to play Warhammer. As a recovering addict, you're going to need community to get well.

Even if you can afford other amenities, you need a community at your back. It's awesome to have great medical supervision, to see a good therapist, and to have the encouragement of friends, but that isn't enough. You need a die-hard group of people who experience the same reality to lean on to keep you emotionally and spiritually well. Church may be enough for some people, but if you're reading this book, chances are that's not a viable route. It's not for me.

What I really miss about church is the sense of security, in mind, body, and spirit. I knew if there were anything I needed, it would be provided. I'd never be without a place to stay at night, and I'd never go hungry. There were always people to be around, and they loved me for just being myself. Unfortunately, at seventeen I didn't believe in God anymore and felt like I was living a lie, so I left the church. I'd never been more alone.

The church I was in when I was a kid encompassed my whole life. Maybe some of you are thinking of the church you visited a couple of times a year; I was at church or related activities many times per week. For three teenage years, I joined a cult and was lucky to get out when I did. I tried to go back to normal churches, but they didn't work for me anymore. All of my conscious time since the age of four had been spent knowing I'd be a preacher someday. That dream was over.

I'd been rattled by years of cult life. While other teenagers were out racing cars and losing their virginity, I was evangelizing at Boston's subway stops and fighting other cults for recruiting territory. I had missed out on all the normal teenage socialization.

I found my way to the Bay Area punk scene like a dog lost on a family vacation finds its way home. I was anything but normal, and so was the punk scene. The scene was full of kids with shitty home lives and weird backgrounds. By being all fucked up, I fit in.

A few years later, I found the underground poetry scene. This is the group of poets who immediately predated the slam era, and some of whom made up its first generation of performers. Confessional and transgressive writing were very popular. The more I wrote against religion and about my messed-up childhood, the more welcome I became.

Intertwined with the poetry scene of San Francisco was a performance art scene. Ever wonder what a stripper does on her day off? She dresses up like a sexy Statue of Liberty and sings an alternate version of the national anthem. Also included were theater rejects who were unable to work with others, trust-funders who went off their meds, and guys who like to stick foreign objects up their asses in front of a crowd of people who paid $10 a head to get in. I was the most well-adjusted person out of everyone. Weird religions were like the minor leagues for this crowd.

What all of these scenes offered me was community. I did like the music and the poetry, but the purpose they really served in my life was providing me with a social group of like-minded people. Being a recovering addict and not hanging out with other like people is akin to being a punk and never going to shows and only hanging out with jocks; if I told you to do that, you'd think I was insane. This is what it sounds like to me when someone says he wants to stay clean and sober on his own.

12 Step and Atheists

Atheists bore me—all they ever talk about is God.
—Heinrich Böll, *The Clown*

The last place I wanted to go was to a church, but that's where most of the 12-Step meetings were. Churches remind me of every bad moment from my childhood. Everyone swore to me it wouldn't be a problem, but it was still hard for me.

God, with reference to 12 Step, can be anything you want it to be. It's a god of your understanding. No one will tell you in 12 Step to believe in a specific god. They will even tell you that you don't have to call it that.

The problem with this is that all of the qualities ascribed to the 12-Step God only describe one God ever in the history of theology: the Protestant Christian God. God is aware of you, and you can directly communicate with it, and it can remove your defects of character. Past the age of the patriarchs in the Old Testament, God talked only to select leaders and the clergy. With the coming of the New Testament, Christ introduced the idea of prayer as a direct communication with

God. The Catholic Church introduced the idea that one cannot confess sins for forgiveness except through a priest. The Protestants brought back direct communication with God for purposes of redemption. No other religion has this simple method. In many religions, the people are too small for their god to even be aware of their existence; priests, sacrifices, and offerings must be there for the gods to take notice.

Also, at the end of many 12-Step meetings, I've heard the Lord's Prayer read, which is text from the New Testament in which Jesus Christ teaches his apostles how to pray. It doesn't apply to any other religion at all.

Some people make up their own God. This is the most pretentious idea of all, that we as simple creations could have an understanding of our superior creator, to the point that we construct the God ourselves.

Every time I'd try to talk about these points after a meeting, I always managed to upset other people. It's as if they were being told they weren't real. It's a common misconception about atheists that we are trying to convince the world that we are right and everyone else is wrong; the majority of religions work this way. It doesn't do much good to try to explain to a religious person that atheists think we're right, but we're not saying that anyone else is wrong. Maybe I'm wrong about atheism and there is a deistic being, so why would I try to convince anyone else about my opinion? It's really hard for religious people to distance themselves from the religion to talk to someone about atheism.

For me, talking to Christians about atheism has been much like talking to people who think that pro wrestling is real. I can give them facts, present them with rational arguments, but they refuse to even ponder the idea that everything they know is wrong. The idea of it can really upset them. If you are an atheist, I suggest not bringing it up at all.

So what's an atheist to do? I struggled with this idea for years, stuck on Steps 2 and 3. But I wasn't going to give up until I found the answer. I used to quit things when they became too difficult or seemed to be a futile effort. I made up my mind not to quit until I found a better program. I didn't find another. What I did find are non-deistic Higher Powers that have worked quite well for me.

The Ideal Image

With the Ideal Image, your Higher Power is the person you want to be. Praying to yourself means that you are reaffirming your desire to become closer to your Ideal Image.

Who's the person you wanted to be? What qualities did you think you had when you were drunk or high?

When I was drunk, I felt like people liked me more, that I fit in to any situation, that people were glad to have me around. In dangerous situations, I wasn't afraid. It was easier for me to socialize in general, but specifically to talk to women I liked.

When I got sober, I didn't know how I would be any of these things I had been when I was loaded. I wrote down all the ways I thought I was when I was drunk. There was nothing on the list that was out of my reach. All I needed was the courage and self-confidence to access them.

I spent much of my newfound time with a clear mind to think about what I really wanted for myself, about the qualities I admired in other people, and what I wanted to achieve in my one lifetime. I came up with my Ideal Image. I wanted to be an important writer of American literature, to be remembered and studied long after my death. I wanted a long-term relationship with a woman who was good for me, kindhearted, and would be with me as I grew through my changes, someone whom I could look up to for encouragement and advice. I wanted to rebuild the friendships that I had let decay through isolation and my own distancing. I wanted not only to be a better stage performer, but one of the best ever, like my heroes George Carlin, Richard Pryor, and Bill Hicks. I wanted to regain my physical health: I had become overweight and had done much damage to my gastrointestinal system. I wanted to go back to making $40K a year, not a princely salary by any means, but enough to meet my needs and still have some money left over for fun.

Decide what you want for yourself, physically, emotionally, socially, and sexually. Make a list. Be specific. Don't say you want a lot of money; find a specific number. Is it a million dollars? Would $900,000 do? Figure out exactly where you want to be, the same way you knew exactly what kind of booze you liked to drink, or how many grams of coke you wanted, or whatever. Think of these specifics as a location to which you are traveling. There is distance between you and these goals.

When other people are praying in meetings, when they say the word *God*, you think of your Ideal Image. Your sobriety will help you achieve every single one of these things. You will be surprised how quickly some of them come, and then you'll be frustrated as others take time. But I guarantee that working the steps is the key to being who you want to be.

Just as others pray daily, you should think to yourself daily about what you can do to be closer to this Ideal Image. Think: "What can I do today to make my life better?" "What can I do to become more like my Ideal Image?"

The Baby Odin Never Cries

Christian children are often frightened with the weird line, "Every time you ___, it makes the Baby Jesus cry." Not only is that a cruel thing to say to a child, it makes little sense. For this to be true, there would have to be a Jesus in a static baby form that is somehow connected to the sins of small children everywhere. Baby Jesus was only a baby in human form, not in a deistic form. Even as a child, I didn't buy this one.

The idea of there being "God babies" always struck me as a weird one. I could only picture a little Satan and a little Jesus in diapers on some Saturday morning cartoon. So I came up with the idea of the Baby Odin.

The Baby Odin is a badass. Unlike your Baby Jesus, who cries more than the front row of a Morrissey concert, the Baby Odin never cries. The Baby Odin can watch *Old Yeller, Where the Red Fern Grows,* and *Brian's Song* back to back to back and not quiver a lip. No matter what you do, the Baby Odin never cries.

I heard someone use Odin in the place of God in my Tuesday night men's meeting, and it stuck in my head. *This guy can't really believe in Odin, can he?* I thought. I had heard some far-out stuff in my time in meetings, but the chief of the Norse gods? Is he really praying to Odin?

I thought about it, and soon the picture of the Baby Odin came into my head. I imagined an angry, one-eyed baby, and couldn't keep myself from laughing. If I had an awesome '70s van, the Baby Odin would definitely be painted on the side of it, instead of a wizard fighting a unicorn or whatever.

Here's the thing: If you have any god at all, the rest of the people in the program will humor you. While the atheist thing seems to set many of them off, if you have any god of your understanding, they will accept it as your Higher Power. It doesn't matter if it is as ridiculous as the Baby Odin, everyone will accept it. So if you need to get people off your back about the atheist problem, this will likely work.

Thoughts on the Serenity Prayer

God, grant me the serenity to accept the things I cannot change, the courage to change the things I can, and the wisdom to know the difference.

God

As covered in this chapter, the 12 Steppers don't mean "God," although it's what they say. I have my Ideal Image; and he and I are distant in many ways. I'm speaking to an esoteric me, or a me from the future, to remind me that I'm trying to be a Me I'm Not Yet.

Serenity

What is serenity, other than an inappropriate name for a stripper? From the prayer, you're going to need serenity before you accept the things you cannot change. But also, from the request, you can assume that you as an addict do not have it in a natural state. So what is your natural state? Chaos!

Chaos!

Beautiful chaos, the bully, the jester, the tempter, the sucker-punching, pants-kicking, wind-knocking imp that rules your life. It's the wind that breaks your wings.

Chaos is what ruined your drug run. It's the cop's flashlight while you're fixing in the car. It's the dye bomb in the sack of stolen bank money. It's the burst pipe from the upstairs neighbor's apartment that soaks a table full of cocaine while you're splitting the kilo into ounces.

> **What is serenity, other than an inappropriate name for a stripper?**

On a smaller, more mundane scale, chaos is the flow of little things that made the simple instances of the day into a bizarre situation. Chaos is the angry roommate, the nagging landlord, the car that breaks down more than it runs. Chaos is the natural state of the addict.

Getting back to the concept of serenity. . . . Serenity is the opposite of that chaos. Telling an addict who is freaking out to calm down does no good. Telling a recovering addict to relax and not worry also does no good. The world of an addict is a crazy world, but it's home; the world of a recovering addict is differently crazy, but it's a foreign crazy, for which there are no emotional coping mechanisms.

The best way I can describe serenity to a recovering addict is to talk about it in drug terms. Serenity is that high you've been chasing after all these years. Say what you want about physiology, but to me, the addict makes that monogamous vice choice after a moment of calm is experienced while high.

Let's look at this from the point of view of the alcoholic. I'm going to exclude drug addicts for this illustration, since they rarely have a choice between brands unless they're in a medical marijuana club. The alcoholic, in early stages, drinks whatever he or she gets hold of, sometimes vile choices made in the desperation of access: teenagers drink whatever is ignored in the parent's liquor cabinet, whatever is at the party, or whatever is easiest to steal from the store. In mid-stage, the alcoholic buys his or her own liquor, with a favorite of each kind: a favorite beer, vodka, whiskey, or tequila. In later stages, the alcoholic often has selected a single choice, and other drinks will not do.

At my end, I drank only bourbon. There was a serenity I was chasing by getting drunk many nights; years before, that moment of calm had long since left me. I was never drunk enough, no matter how much I had. But it wasn't always like that.

In the beginning of my drinking years, there was a peace of mind that came with inebriation. I was in the moment, feeling good, with friends around me. All the pain I'd been carrying for years went away with only a few drinks. But when it stopped working, I refused to acknowledge that I hadn't enjoyed drinking for a long time. I kept thinking it was something else—ironically those things in my life I thought drinking helped me to enjoy, like the company of my friends. Increasingly I drank alone in my house. That peace of mind never came back.

That peace of mind is the serenity I now strive to achieve. In that mindset, I'm calm enough to accept the world around me. Whether it's a long line at the supermarket full of people who can't make a simple transaction, or an irate customer at work yelling at me over some issue with which I had nothing to do, or a tragedy like the death of a friend, I realize that I don't have to absorb the chaos into myself, that I can maintain peace in the face of random trauma. I am a pond that refuses to ripple no matter how many stones are thrown into it.

Accept the Things I Cannot Change

My first image of an alcoholic was Otis from Mayberry on *The Andy Griffith Show*. Otis, and the rest of his community, accepted his problem so well that he walked into the jail every night and locked himself up. What did I learn from this? Drunks are funny. Years after Ray Milland gave a signature performance in *The Lost Weekend* as a relentless alcoholic, drunks were still funny. Now, drunks are considered sad and pathetic, while stoners are considered hilarious. From Sean Penn's Jeff Spicoli portrayal in *Fast Times at Ridgemont High* to now, the focus of funny addicts has been pinned on the pothead.

It was really easy for me to accept my drinking. Bars exist for the purpose of people who like to drink getting together to do just that. Why not drink at home? Because drinking in a bar is like a party. It's socially acceptable. Everyone does it . . . everyone else in the bar, that is.

But what I couldn't accept was my childhood trauma and the tragedies that dogpiled me later. I split my formative years first as a fundamentalist extremist and later as a cult member. My friends from those years didn't fare well, ending up in psych wards and detention centers. When I got into the art scene in the late '80s, many artists I knew were in advanced stages of AIDS, and soon died. In the early '90s, my younger friends were taken by heroin, crack, and speed, and died from ODs or the chaos that comes from the lifestyle. By the late '90s, I had a graveyard full of dead friends.

> By the late '90s, I had a graveyard full of dead friends.

My anger at these things I could not change fueled many drunken binges, and what I accepted instead was the fact that I had to drink a pint of whiskey to kill the shakes, and another pint to get me to where I wanted to be. There wasn't a part of me that thought two pints of whiskey every day was normal, but my acceptance was generous.

Courage to Change the Things I Can

You're going to need all the courage you can get, because what's changing is the fulcrum on which your life has been balanced. Your relationships, your jobs, your housing have all been determined by your drug and alcohol use. More than that, how you see yourself and how you think the world sees you have your usage in the descriptions. By coming to 12 Step, you're attempting to change a focal point of your life. You have courage, but you've had it in all the wrong places.

What scares you is the mundane parts of life: job interviews, first dates, and dinner parties. These are the minor dramas of life for which you've always had the support of your favorite vice. You think being drunk or high helps in these times. Maybe it has, once or twice, but it's ruined you the rest of the time, no matter what you blamed the failure on. But what you may not realize are the times that you've been a brave addict.

Drug deals, bar fights, and random accidents scare most people, but you live with them like they're your frat brothers. That moment in the drug deal when everyone else thinks you're a cop, squaring off against a guy only to see his three friends get off their barstools, and cutting your leg jumping over a fence a mile from home, all these moments live in the field of frightening possibilities for Normies. For you, it's a series of events for which you are prepared and practiced. If you can survive these episodes, you can surely withstand the rigors of a 12-Step program.

Wisdom to Tell the Difference

Even though it comes third after serenity and courage, you'll need wisdom most of all. This is how you will determine what goes in which category: changeable or unchangeable. To me, it was the most valuable of the three.

Don't confuse wisdom with intelligence. Those are two separate qualities. There are plenty of people who are not that smart who seem to make healthy decisions in life. There are also plenty of smart people who single-handedly ruin careers, relationships, and the surrounding environment with bad decisions. There have been many times in which my bullheaded intelligence told me I was doing the right thing and not to listen to the advice of others. I thought I could always reason my way through any situation with my logistical skills as my weapon. I can learn new processes and techniques quickly, but I have often used this to my destruction, not my betterment.

Chapter 3

Entering:
Get in
Where
You Fit in

I like to group the 12 Steps into three sections so I can think about them in a different way.

Steps 1 through 3 are the *entering* steps. In these steps, we admit that we're an addict and don't want to live this way anymore. Our way made us addicts. Here we announce that we are looking for another way to live.

Steps 4 through 7 are about *internal transformation*. They require taking action to change your personal internal makeup. Steps 4 and 5 are where the "miracle" starts to happen. Step 4 is a big wall for many people to climb over. They don't mind getting clean and sober, but having to change on a spiritual level is a hard one to handle; sometimes we learn that our opinions of the world and how we deal with it emotionally are completely wrong. This is usually a scary step to take, which is why the word *fearless* comes up quickly.

Steps 8 through 12 are about *external transformation*. Once you've become aware of your internal problems, it's time to go out into the world and be your new self. Your new ideas will be put into play when you encounter people from your past, as you deal with people in your present, and as you take initiative to reach out to and help others.

Step 1: Admitting What All Your Friends Already Know

We admitted we were powerless over alcohol—
that our lives had become unmanageable.

Unmanageable

Unmanageable was my magic word. That's the word I heard at my first meeting that made me feel like I belonged there.

My life could've gotten much worse. Relative to many other people I've met, I have what's often called a "high bottom." When I bottomed out, it was much less traumatic than other addicts' experiences were. But you don't have to lose every single thing you care about to be an alcoholic; it's that you can't handle what you still have.

I lived in a house. I had a hot girlfriend. I had cable. I had shoes. These were all things, that, according to my logic, alcoholics don't have. Alcoholics live in the park, or in a cardboard box. Alcoholics are alone in the world. Alcoholics don't get to watch *The Sopranos* every Sunday night. When I passed out in my Pumas every night, no one stole them off my feet. But my life was far from manageable.

The house I lived in was a condemnable property by any inspector's standards. The house was a notorious punk house in Oakland, full of kids barely into their twenties. They got drunk and high on a regular basis, but this is a vestige of youth that you either quit while you're young or you become an addict if you don't die. If you are the Old Guy In The Punk House, move out. You have a substance abuse problem.

I'm not sure why my girlfriend was with me, other than she had a thing for fuckups. Her other boyfriends had been drunks or unemployable freaks, and I fit both of those descriptions. Over the years, I dated women with alcoholic fathers and many other addicts. Because they were overcompensatingly beautiful, I felt that this made me look to the outsider like I was a guy with it all.

> **Many nights that I thought I was "writing" I merely had my computer on while getting wasted to the sounds of HBO movies.**

The cable I had was stolen. I stole it from my upstairs neighbors, who had stolen it in the first place. I didn't get all the channels. I only got up to forty channels. I didn't feel that it was my place to complain, however. Many nights that I thought I was "writing" I merely had my computer on while getting wasted to the sounds of HBO movies.

My shoes were fucked up. They were little more than leather slippers. It wasn't that I couldn't afford another pair. But spending even $40 on shoes may have precluded me from buying two fifths of my favorite whiskey.

Don't get me wrong—I lost a lot of things I wanted in my life because I was a drunk. I had dropped out of school, saying it was too hard to work my way through, when in reality I prioritized going out every night over studying. Many good women I dated broke it off with me when they realized how much I drank. There were many manuscripts started but few completed, making it impossible for me to get a second book published. Club bookers and promoters knew that I could be a hassle to deal with, either because of my temper or my unreliability, which cost me many gigs. There were jobs that I performed really well but was let go from, and while it was never explicitly stated that it was because of my drinking, I can only assume that that was the "no reason" that I got let go, or not promoted. But I didn't see the glass as half-empty. No, it was definitely half-full—half-full of whiskey. I kept finding things I had that proved I wasn't an alcoholic.

The word *unmanageable* made perfect sense to me. Every little task in my life felt like a trial of Hercules. Paying bills on time, making it to the unemployment office by 4 p.m., everything seemed really complicated. I couldn't manage anything in my life. As I looked around the room full of people, when they said "unmanageable," I thought that word fit better than any other word to describe my life.

Powerless

This sounds a bit strong at first. Powerless? I don't think so! I'm not one of those winos who drank himself out of his mind and his home! But many were the nights I tried not to drink "too much," that I swore to stop before I blacked out, or thought I would stick to beer and not touch the whiskey, and it all went to shit. When I started drinking, I didn't stop until I ran out of access to alcohol, by lack of money, lack of charm, or lack of consciousness. That's powerless over alcohol.

There's this old joke around the drug scene where someone says, "I hate cocaine. Got any?" With cigarettes, coke, crack, and heroin, the powerless principle plays more into effect than with other substances. But it happens as well with booze, pot, coffee, and sugar. It's a joke when someone eats too many cookies, but the principle remains. We are people who can't control ourselves around certain things. If you're drinking, eating, or smoking more than you really want to, it has power over you.

Step 2: Give Sanity a Chance

*Came to believe that a Power greater
than ourselves could restore us to sanity.*

Sanity is madness put to good uses.
—George Santayana, *Little Essays*

Steps 2 and 3 are the most treacherous for the atheist. These are going to take a lot of patience with yourself and the outside world.

Sanity

When I first saw Step 2 on the wall, I thought, *What do you mean, "restore"? Do I have to admit that I'm insane now?* Well, you are insane, most likely. But calm down. The word doesn't mean as much as you may think it does.

Our society has really stigmatized the word *insane*. We think of padded walls, straightjackets, and Napoleon hats. We think of the movie *Sybil*. We think of people wandering the streets muttering to themselves. But we shouldn't think of insanity as such an extreme.

Being sane means you have a sound mind and make rational decisions. Making rational decisions implies that you are working with a proper set of priorities. There isn't an addict out there who has a proper set of priorities. Welcome to insanity.

Think about it. When you've gambled the rent money, or you've spent it on cocaine. When you have some kind of system for drinking that never works, but always ends up with you in full blackout mode, and you insist on using the system or tweaking it.

You've had jobs that allow you to stay out late at bars. You've had jobs that needed you to stay up all night. You've had jobs that required isolation. You've gotten all these jobs to enable your usage. You've passed up better jobs and opportunities that you knew wouldn't allow you to get high, drunk, or stoned during work. Have you ever applied for a job that has regular drug testing?

On the note of drug testing, if you've ever used some method to cheat a drug test, you're an addict. If you've ever brought in someone else's urine, swallowed weird concoctions that supposedly clean your bloodstream, or used any devices bought from the back pages of *High Times* magazine, you're an addict. If you can't go without cocaine and marijuana when you know you're going to be tested and your job depends on it, you're an addict. Normal people who aren't allowed to smoke pot by their jobs don't smoke pot. If you like getting high better than getting your paycheck, you're an addict.

Your romantic relationships have priorities that were set by your usage. Your partners have been codependent enablers. Your partners have been other addicts. Your partners have been the children of addicts. Your partners have fled in terror when they found out how much you used, but you blamed them for "not being able to take your intensity." Maybe you're good on that first date to the bar, but when you have to go on later dates, you can't stand how boring they are.

Your friendships revolve around your usage. Your best friends are the guys from the bar. There's a guy in your posse that you don't like, but you tolerate him since he always has the coke. When your normal friends settle down and "get boring," you never see them anymore; you don't understand why they can't come out to the bar just because they have a kid or two. Do you have a friend whose favorite drink you know but a name you can't remember?

As you can see, your life has been prioritized around your drug and alcohol use, whether it was professionally, romantically, or socially. This is why these things are unsatisfying to you, and you use them as an excuse or a reason to get high.

If this is at all familiar to you, trust me: it's insane behavior.

Step 3: Surrender—It's Not Just a Cool Cheap Trick Song

Made a decision to turn our will and our lives over to the care of God as we understood Him.

Whether it's called The Will of God, Fate, Destiny, Karma, or whatever else, there are aspects of the universe that are beyond our control. People of various religions make their will known to their supreme beings, and they have accepted they will not always get what they want. People pray, meditate, make sacrifices . . . but it's all the same. They are making their desires into a specific statement. They know exactly what they want out of life, and exactly what they are grateful for.

This abandonment of control to a Higher Power is what most religions call *faith*. Faith is a powerful human attribute. While I may not believe that it's a deistic being that makes faith work, I do believe that faith has a positive effect on our lives.

Faith has a power we may never understand. There is the feeling of being in a crowd that all believe the same thing, whether it's a crowd at a church, a political protest, or a rock concert. Being a part of that group dynamic is a great feeling. Why is it easier for a sports team to win at home than away? Does it have to do with the 50,000 people exerting their will simultaneously on the game? Perhaps.

All religions of the world have two things in common: they're based on stories, and there's an extent to which these stories are believed as truths. Every religion has stories as part of its core; you're told stories that are used as a basis for the doctrines and tenets of the religion. Without those stories, there wouldn't be a reason to believe anything you heard. But the story is presented as a sort of proof that the religion has validity. Your belief in the stories, in the religion, and the existence of the cosmic structure portrayed therein is also faith.

Outside of religion, stories can still have a healing effect. Storytelling predates written language and religion. Humans love stories. Humans want to believe in ideas and heroes. This is what gives us hope and strength to live our lives. Whether it's the Epic of Gilgamesh or the *Star Wars* movies, we love to watch, read, or hear about those like us who face an unbeatable foe and somehow emerge the victor.

There's no scientific proof of my next opinion, but listen up, because I'm right anyway: The stories we tell each other have real healing power. That's why there are stories in church, in kindergarten, and in 12-Step meetings. On a base level of development, humans get a lot of spiritual and emotional healing from storytelling. We need stories to heal our non-physical selves and give us direction in which to grow. If you're wondering what could ever possibly take the pain away, what would quell the depression, or what would relieve the anxiety once you quit using, trust me, it's the stories.

◇◇◇

What I'm getting at is that religions can work if you really believe with all your heart and mind that they do. But if you have a bit of doubt, it won't work. I'm not saying religions work for the reasons the practicers say they do, I'm saying by faith and group consciousness, people have the power to change themselves and push their reality in a different direction.

Let me put it this way: The difference between the Bible and a Magic Eightball is that four hundred years ago, you would've been burned at the stake for owning the Magic Eightball. It would have been considered black magick at the time, because people would have believed it really worked. I think that now, if someone truly believed in that toy, and used it every single time with consistency, it would have an overall positive effect on his or her life. I'm not saying it does work; I'm saying it *can* work. Got me?

Own Power, Outer Power, and Line of Control

Here's another way I think of the cosmic structure: with a trinity of Own Power, Outer Power, and the Line of Control.

Your Own Power is what is within your control. Are you going to a meeting today? Are you going to bet on a football game? Are you going to send a résumé to that company?

Outer Power is every part of life that is outside of your control. You can bet on the football game, but you can't determine the outcome. You can call that number, but you don't know if you'll get a date. You can buy the stock, but you have no effect on its performance.

The Line of Control is what separates these two powers. It's an ever-moving boundary. Say you find $100 on the street when you are flat broke; the Line of Control moves immediately. You may now control what meal you buy next, but you can't control how well it's cooked.

Acknowledgment of the Line of Control brings me a lot of inner peace in my life. I see what lies on which side of the line and strive to only concern myself with what is within my own power. It's easier to see that I can expand the area of my Own Power. Every time I spend my money wisely, use my time wisely, and treat those near me with compassion and respect, I broaden the area of my Own Power.

Chapter 4

Internal Transformation: You're a Sick Puppy

Step 4: Get Over Your Own Bullshit

*Made a searching and fearless
moral inventory of ourselves.*

*Too many people overvalue what they are not
and undervalue what they are.*
—Malcolm S. Forbes

There's plenty on this in the Big Book, but it's still not complete. You need to do more than what it says in the book to get to yourself completely.

Step 4 is the step on which most people derail. Take a look at that word *fearless.* It's there for a reason. This step is scary.

What you'll see as a standard inventory item is resentment. In making a resentment list, you have to write down everyone about whom you carry negative feelings. Then you include your part in the process, and the end result.

This is a good start. Maybe enough for your first time through the steps. But as you get to Step 10, when you'll come back to this point, you'll find you're still lacking.

A moral inventory includes all morality, not just resentments. If you're a member of a religion, your morality is likely defined by your religious denomination. While I've met plenty of religious people who don't seem to care about the particulars of their own religion, I don't understand that at all. When I was a member of a religion, I took its moral stances very seriously as absolute right and wrongs. That's up to you to figure out, if you are like that. But if you're an atheist, now's the time to define your own morality. This is a very important process in your recovery. Take it seriously.

Atheism and Moral Inventories

Before you make any judgments about yourself, simply describe your history. It's an inventory, after all. Do nothing more than go through the warehouse of your past conduct. The literature talks mainly about resentment with this step. Also, a sexual inventory is common. But that's not nearly enough. You really need a full inventory of your morality. I've made some suggestions.

Stealing

In the first of three columns, list every item you've ever taken, no matter how small, that you did not pay for or return. In the second column, name the owner of the item. In the third column, describe the reason you stole it.

I'm guessing the third column is mostly filled with "Needed Money for Drug Habit." And, as booze is much easier to steal than drugs, there's likely "Needed Booze" in there as well.

Is it okay to steal from a large corporate store? How about a small neighborhood store? From someone you don't know who is rich? From someone who won't notice?

Fidelity

I've asked sponsees to list in their sexual inventories the times they cheated on their girlfriends or wives. Most of the time, they don't come up with anything. It's not because they haven't cheated. It's because their definition of what is cheating is all screwed up.

Especially since Bill Clinton's scandal, there are a lot of guys who would say that getting oral sex isn't cheating. There are some other guys who think that it isn't cheating if a condom is worn. There are guys who will have sex with another woman but not kiss her, because that would be cheating. Some consider that if they pay for sex, it's not cheating. I've heard these specific things mentioned in all seriousness.

Instead of a list here, write down specific ideas of what you think being faithful to a partner is and what the boundaries are. Be sure to include what behavior you expect in return.

I can't list here what is right and wrong; you'll have to decide that for yourself. But you will need to get a clear picture of who you are relationship-wise and find someone else who accepts your standards, and you need to accept his or hers.

Just because *you* don't think of an action as cheating doesn't mean your partner doesn't. Chances are, you haven't been around a long-term healthy relationship, ever. I'd wager you have dated other addicts or the children of addicts. The rules in such codependent relationships are very different from those of normal relationships.

Honesty and Integrity

I think of honesty as being truthful to others, and integrity as being truthful to yourself.

After a career of acquiring and using drugs, it's easy to lie without even thinking about it. It may be a natural state to which you've conditioned yourself. You may be constantly coming up with stories that are better than the truth. This has to stop. Even if you think it's harmless. Even if it really is mostly harmless. When the Normies find out, it will freak them out that you lie about little things like what you had for lunch or what you watched on TV last night. They won't trust you with the bigger issues even if you are telling the truth about them.

An honesty inventory from the past could be impossible. But keep track of a current inventory. Do you lie? At all? To whom? For what reason? What fear provokes the untruth? Even if they're little lies that seem insignificant to you, you need to find out why you tell them. Why not tell the truth?

General Questions to Ask Yourself Throughout Inventory

How did drugs and alcohol play into changing your ideas of what is right and wrong? Can you remember what you thought was acceptable before your usage started? How would you like it to be now?

Step 5: You're Not a Snitch If It's About Yourself

Admitted to God, to ourselves, and to another human being the exact nature of our wrongs.

Do yourself a favor, and admit the exact nature of your wrongs to more than one human being. Really. One's not enough. Can you fathom two? One person in the program, and the other a Normie.

What's the point of this step? Once you read off a list of your resentments, most of them will sound really stupid. You'll realize they shouldn't matter to you, and magically, they won't matter to you anymore.

The other thing that happens is that you start to see how your inventories match up to those of other people. It will give you a chance to observe your own moral code objectively.

By the way, this is going to sound like high comedy to anyone but you. Really, when you hear about the shit people carry around from grade school, you'll understand. So don't get too bent out of shape when you admit the exact nature of your wrongs and people laugh their asses off. Trust me, it's funny. Maybe not yet, but it will be.

Step 6: Nobody's Perfect, Especially Not You

*Were entirely ready to have God
remove all these defects of character.*

Once you've done your fourth and fifth steps, your sixth shouldn't be that hard to start. But there is often a reluctance to let go of some of your character defects. A lot of them are fun. But maybe gambling, hookers, and strip clubs aren't the best activities for you.

First, you have to determine what your character defects are. If you don't know what these defects are, go back to Step 4

> **Sometimes, it's not the defect that has to be removed but an attribute that needs to be used in a different way.**

and repeat 4 and 5. It should be clear to you where you're lacking morally.

I think people skip through this step too quickly. I think that often Step 6, then Step 7, are mentally completed but not emotionally completed. It's one thing to think logically that you shouldn't gamble anymore; it's another thing to be entirely ready to never do it again.

I'm using gambling as an example here, because I've seen a lot of men transfer addiction from drugs to gambling. I've also seen it transfer to porn, strippers, and compulsive sex. With women, overeating often happens as well.

What I've seen happen most often is that the addiction goes away, and one of these defects of character becomes stronger. What was before a number-two priority becomes a number-one priority. The guy who liked to get drunk and get into fights will get sober and get into more fights if he doesn't see his rage and anger as defects of character.

Attributes or Defects?

The idea of attributes versus defects has long intrigued me. I thought, *What if that defect is an unalterable part of my personality? What if I can't have it removed?*

Sometimes, it's not the defect that has to be removed, but an attribute that needs to be used in a different way. It's like the villains in comic books always using their powers for evil instead of for good. They could have easily been heroes if they'd lived differently. But hey, radiation blasts can make a guy a little cranky.

Take loyalty, for example. Who doesn't want a loyal friend? My best friends are the ones who stuck by me when times were tough and I wasn't that great of a guy to be around. I treasure their loyalty. But it's not always a good thing to be a loyal person, right?

There's the kind of person who stays in an abusive relationship out of loyalty. That's no good. Instead of using all that energy in a positive manner, they're using it in what is ultimately a self-destructive manner. My feelings of letting "The Boys" down if I quit was my weird sense of loyalty coming into play.

Spontaneity is the same thing as unreliability, as are self-confidence and too much pride. There are many examples of this. Think of anyone close to you. The flip side of the qualities you like about him or her is what makes you crazy as well.

Step 7: Taking Out the Emotional Trash

Humbly asked Him to remove our shortcomings.

Humility. Where to start with this one? Humility shows up in Step 7, but then it's gone. If I were to rewrite the Serenity Prayer, I would definitely throw in something about "Grant me the humility to get through the fucking day."

Humility is a huge problem for me. I define humility as not thinking that myself *or my needs* are more important than anyone else. My lack of humility is definitely a defect of character.

Most people think they're humble. But addiction erodes how we value humility. This lack of humility is at the core of an addict's debilitated morality.

Initially, when we're getting loaded, we think that what we do does not affect other people. It's not about how it affects our families and friends. It's about ourselves. This is the first phase of our lack of humility. It's bad enough here, but it gets worse.

Next, we may see our need to get high as more important than others' needs to own their own property. Whether it's scamming or shoplifting from a large corporation or smashing the window of someone's car to steal the CDs under the driver's seat, it's stealing. Stealing doesn't seem right before the addiction sets in. Why? Because we automatically think we wouldn't like it if people stole from us. We see other people as equals. When we think we're better, more important, or that our needs are more urgent, it's easy to rationalize the behavior. It gets worse from this point.

At some point, we steal drugs from our other drug buddies. There's some unspoken honor in the fact that you don't rip off your friends in your drug circle, even if you are all a bunch of unabashed thieves. All kinds of weird acts are forgiven in this group: physical and emotional abuse, infidelity, violence, but when you steal someone's shot, you've committed an unforgivable sin. Junkies will curse your name and warn the entire neighborhood. You will wear a Scarlet Letter for this one.

It's not only about stealing. This is what makes drunks think it's okay to drive home. It's that me-first mindset that you have to lose. There are a lot of actions you may take that you think have no effect on other people, but the consequences reach further than you realize.

Chapter 5

External Transformation: The World Is Big and Scary

Steps 8 and 9: Start Writing, This Is Going to Take a While

Made a list of all persons we had harmed,
and became willing to make amends to them all; and,
Made direct amends to such people wherever possible,
except when to do so would injure them or others.

These are the steps everyone knows about. What the typical person knows is that the guy in recovery is supposed to go around to everyone and apologize for his rash action. It's in popular culture and film and TV, portrayed not for 12-Step reasons but for other reasons in *My Name Is Earl*. Making amends is a setup for many sitcom episodes.

Don't let it be a setup for you, too. Take your time getting here. I see too many people rushing to make amends. There are seven other steps for you to complete first.

A lot of men take some kind of pleasure in admitting wrongdoing and apologizing for it. It's the same kind of guy who brags at work on Monday about how much he threw up on Saturday night. There's an odd exhibitionist side of this step. But it's not supposed to be for you as much as it is for other people.

It's common for a guy to want to call up his old girlfriends first. Really, this isn't an excuse to call the woman who told you never to call again. In the back of his mind, there's many a man who thinks that when she sees him with all of his shit together, she'll screw him on the porch. That is not the ninth step, that's an attempt to get laid. Don't even think about approaching the exes with only an apology in tow; you'd better be ready on the spot with all the cash you owe.

In order to really do the eighth and ninth steps well, you need to thoroughly do all the previous steps. You need a firm grasp on your defects of character and an as-complete-as-possible moral inventory. Without having done these well, you won't understand what your part in it all was, or how you've changed internally so you don't want to live this way anymore.

You need to be really emotionally and spiritually strong at this point. Some people you encounter will still be pissed off at you. If you're still prone to fighting or if you still have a prideful need to be right all the time, you're not eighth- and ninth-step ready.

Next are what I think are the three most important steps, and the ones fewest people outside recovery programs know about.

Step 10: Lather, Rinse, Repeat

Continued to take personal inventory and when we were wrong promptly admitted it.

Step 10 talks about continuing to take a moral inventory. Hey, guess what? You're not done yet. This step says that through-out your life, as you wise up and learn about yourself, you'll realize that no matter how thorough you thought your fourth step was, it wasn't nearly done. There is a lot more in you that needs explaining.

This is the "lather, rinse, repeat" (the directions on every bottle of shampoo if you've ever bothered to read them) step of the 12 Steps. The bad news: your step work is never done. The good news: it's no more complicated than washing your hair. The inventory is a beast the first time you put it together, but you really complete it throughout your life as you continue in your recovery.

> **The bad news: your step work is never done. The good news: it's no more complicated than washing your hair.**

Step 11: Pray Faster

Sought through prayer and meditation to improve our conscious contact with God as we understood Him, praying only for knowledge of His will for us and the power to carry that out.

For the atheist, improving your conscious contact with God is really coming to terms with the person you are and who the world outside of you is. Truly understanding your impact on the world is the epiphany for the atheist. Internally, you will have an clear idea of your self-image, to the point of having specific goals for yourself. Externally, you will understand what futures are within your control and which ones are beyond your control. Most important, you will attain an inner peace that most people never find in one lifetime.

Where it says "through prayer and meditation," I read, "through creation and performance," as those are the God-actions in my life. When I'm writing at home, I'm improving my knowledge of the self. When I take the writing into public and perform it, I improve my understanding of the outside world. I can't tell you what your God-actions will be. That's part of your own journey.

In the late '80s punk scene, it was common to hear people yell "play faster!" at shows. This is the "pray faster!" step. Whatever you're doing to reconcile your spiritual well-being, do more of it as you go. You wouldn't lift the same weights in the gym all your life; you would increase the sets, repetitions, or weight. Just the same, you should occasionally reevaluate your life, goals, and accomplishments, and how they relate to your recovery.

Step 12: Get This—You Matter!

Having had a spiritual awakening as the result of
these steps, we tried to carry this message to alcoholics,
and to practice these principles in all our affairs.

I thought I had most of 12 Step figured out. The whole thing seemed pretty clear to me. After about three years, I felt good about myself and thought I had a firm grasp on all twelve steps. But it was that pesky twelfth step that was lurking in the shadows for me, and it snuck up on me not once, but twice.

The first time the importance of Step 12 snuck up on me was when I got my first sponsee. I was hanging out at my favorite meeting after it was over. I can't remember what the topic was, but I do remember that I was feeling the euphoria that comes with the group consciousness. Without the meetings, I tend to isolate too much and it's bad for me. A positive group experience feeds my hungry extroverted parts. Then this kid came up to me and my immediate circle of friends, and said he needed a sponsor.

Carlos was in his mid-twenties and was in the Salvation Army's Adult Rehabilitation Center (ARC). He had been a gangbanger in the Central Valley before getting incarcerated.

"I need a sponsor," he said.

I knew what his problem was. Most people don't want to sponsor the ex-cons. They're intimidating. They condition themselves to look scary. It takes years for them to lose this demeanor that keeps them safe while locked up. As a sponsor, you have to tell people what to do. You have to come down on them, tell them when they are fucking up, tell them that they have to do the step work.

Barnaby looked around the group. He went around in a circle and asked how many sponsees everyone had. Everyone had multiple ones. I had none.

"He's yours," Barnaby said.

"I've never done it before," I said. I was immediately in backpedal mode. Instinctively, I wanted out of it. More responsibility? I don't think so.

"He's yours," Barnaby repeated.

I looked back at Carlos. Underneath the prison tats on his face was a young man asking for help. Guys like him have a hard time asking anyone for help; the fear of showing weakness is learned early on. I knew if he had the courage and the desire to ask me for help, there was no way I could say no.

I worked with Carlos for a few weeks. Then he brought another friend of his, Mike, a scrawny white kid from San Bernardino.

"Mike needs a sponsor," Carlos told me.

"I don't know if I have time for another one," I said. Then I noticed a fresh scar on Mike's neck. "How did you get that scar?" I asked.

"I was tweaking for seven days, and wanted to kill myself, so I cut my throat open with a box cutter and took an Oxycontin. I woke up in the hospital."

"You're in," I told him.

Suddenly, I had two sponsees. There was a *vato* and a tweaker under my care. I had to help these guys get their shit together. They'd both be released from the ARC soon, and what would they do without a good foundation?

I worked with the two of them until they graduated the ARC. While I was working with them, I realized there were a lot of people left off my resentment inventory that I needed to include. While explaining what defects of character were to them, I saw some parts of myself I didn't like. Until I tried to take other people through the steps, I didn't see the full effect of working them.

Right before Carlos left to go back to the Central Valley, he stopped me outside a meeting and thanked me. Maybe you've never been thanked by an ex-con, but they don't throw around gratitude unless they really mean it. I saw him again, remembered the way he used to look, with the fear now gone and replaced by hope.

It hit me that I mattered. After all this time, it took a badass *vato* to remind me of something I knew as a child but forgot along the way. I matter. My life matters. The lives of people around me may be positively or negatively affected by my actions. There is meaning in life, but I'm going to have to create it for myself.

> **I looked back at Carlos. Underneath the prison tats on his face was a young man asking for help.**

◇◇◇

The second time Step 12 snuck up on me was when I secretaried my first meeting. This was another time that it was decided for me that I should do it. This time, with my experience with my sponsees in hindsight, I knew that I should readily accept the task given to me. It was at my Tuesday night men's meeting once again.

It was time for our secretary to step down and for us to vote on another. When I say "vote," it's about the same way that a drill sergeant votes for the private to do push-ups. They voted me in immediately after the current secretary nominated me. I didn't get a chance to say no. The nomination went up, followed by every single one of their hands.

Being the secretary of that meeting was a full-circle experience for me. I had just passed five years sober. I reflected on my half decade of sobriety. I thought back to that first time that I walked in to the meeting and thought everyone was a jackass. I still thought they were jackasses, but they were now *my* jackasses, and I was a jackass, too.

There were a lot of contributing factors to my sobriety, but the sense of community I got from those men every week was my favorite aspect of the entire program. I hadn't felt comfortable being part of a group since I had left the church so many years ago, but I rediscovered how great the group dynamic could be. There was no way the group would let me get away with self-pity or isolation, which have been my worst character defects throughout my life.

What I wasn't prepared for was everyone's eye contact. Mind you, I paid attention during meetings, unlike some who zone out or text message, but even then I was looking at the backs of heads except for the secretary and the speaker. I had more than twenty years of public speaking experience, but it still didn't prepare me for what I saw during my first meeting.

My meeting is full of guys who have done some serious prison time. Many of them are from the adult rehabilitation center down the street, freshly paroled. One of the many ways incarceration affects a man is that it changes his default facial expression; after a while, he has that thousand-yard stare.

Most people in meetings have a default look on their faces, so that they look like zombies. They don't look happy, sad, angry, but rather barely alive. They don't look dead . . . yet. But these guys from prison looked like they were about to kick my ass.

They didn't mean anything by it. That's the way you protect yourself in prison; you look like you're about to go off at any possible moment. I sat at the desk for my first meeting and looked out at forty faces, each one looking more pissed than the last. It freaked me out, but after a few weeks I was used to it.

The lasting effect was more than I could ever have imagined. There's something really special about each and every man in there looking right at me when he shares. I can see the honesty, the hurt, and the victory all at once. Often, I'm the only one who can see it, as no one else looks directly at the one sharing but me.

As I talked to all these men on a weekly basis, it woke up an old part of me that I had shut away in a dark place for a long slumber.

I didn't think I had shut off from the world around me. I had considered myself an emotional and outgoing person. But as I talked to all these men on a weekly basis, it woke up an old part of me that I had shut away in a dark place for a long slumber. I was still isolating—not publicly, but internally.

Over the next year, I really opened up, not just to the men in the group, but to the world around me, to the program, and in my close personal relationships. Out in public, I felt much more of a connection to people I didn't know. I experienced true joy at being a part of a recovery group, especially when newcomers came in the room. And for the first time ever, I was emotionally available to women I was dating.

I had accepted that I wouldn't find a woman who would "get" me. I dated many nice women in sobriety who had interesting lives and were fun to go out with, but I never could make a deep connection. I thought it was because I was too complex or damaged or whatever. Really, though, there was a big part of me still walled off that I never brought out to anyone else.

As I brought out this side of me, my close friendships improved, and I met an awesome woman who really set me on fire. I have a lot more to offer my friends and my girlfriend now: an emotional openness and honesty.

I also made amends to my father. I went to see him over Christmas and apologized for all the stress and anxiety I had caused him when I was a teenager. Previously, I had made amends to him for specific incidents, but I had still never thought about all the weird stress I must have caused him while he worried about whether I was going to live through the weekend. I apologized to him directly, and his reaction was much less than I thought it would be. He more or less shrugged it off, thanked me, and told me it was a long time ago, and that it was all water under the bridge. I thought he would have made a big deal about it. The reason he didn't is that he doesn't hold grudges as tightly as I did. I wanted it to be a whole experience. But that's one of the times when I had to remember that making amends to other people is for them, not for me. Whenever I have a problem, I take it to the group and hear a dozen different opinions on the situation. I usually make it into a topic and throw it out to them. It's like having a roomful of sponsors. I look forward to Tuesdays when I know that any problem I have will be dealt with on a group level. I don't have any reason to keep my drama or problems inside.

> **This is the gift of the twelfth step: the world is a better place for having you in it.**

Best of all is my sense of purpose. As an existentialist atheist, I think there is no grand plan for any one person. If there is going to be meaning in our lives, then we must create it for ourselves. I was content with my purpose as a creative being, an artist, poet, and comedian, sharing my point of view with others. But now I see the joy and inner peace that comes with helping others.

This is the gift of the twelfth step: the world is a better place for having you in it. I used to think that in the grand scheme of time and the existence of humans, it didn't really make a difference if I lived a short drunk life or a long sober one. Now I see that it does, and it's clear to me that though I won't live for the species-span of all humanity, I'll live one life, the best I can.

Chapter 6

Get Off Your Drunk Ass

Goals and the Addict

There is no type of person more goal oriented in the world than the addict. The only goal is to use drugs and/or alcohol. Steps along this way involve acquiring the product or acquiring the means with which to acquire the product. Achieving this goal supersedes friends, family, relationships, jobs, and even physical safety. It's not that the addict cannot achieve goals; it's that the addict only knows how to achieve one goal repeatedly.

> **It's not that the addict cannot achieve goals; it's that the addict only knows how to achieve one goal repeatedly.**

Make Specific Goals

Determine exactly what you want. Not just "money," but how much? Not just "buying a home," but what size and where? Not just "a new job," but what qualities do you want in a job? Unless you know what you're looking for, you won't know it when you see it.

Figure Out Which Goals Should Come First

Would one goal help achieve another? I knew that getting a university degree would help me get a job that would help me achieve financial stability, which would help me get the health care I needed. If you can't figure out the order in the manner of utility, which goals are the quickest to accomplish? Knocking out a few of them quickly will give you momentum to go after your others.

Organize Each Goal into a Series of Steps

Break a goal down into as many steps as possible. If you're forgetful, get a stack of index cards and write a step on each one. This way, you only have to look at one step at a time. You won't be daunted by the complete list of tasks. Also, you get to add in cards when the surprise steps hit you. Carry the card of the step you're working on with you. I added my school cards in with a bunch of other errands and laundry cards. Now I keep a calendar of events through the coming year. But you don't need to start there; planning out your day is a good way to start.

Reevaluate Your Goals

Once you accomplish one goal, you should take a look at your others. What you will find is that achieving goals in your life will open doors for you that you didn't know existed. You may find out about entirely new professions you didn't know about beforehand, or change your ideas about what you want to do with your life. It's okay to change direction; it's only dangerous not to have a direction at all.

Set the Bar Low When You Can

Especially for material goals, a low, attainable goal is best. It's a lot better to start small and have the end be in sight. If it's too high, you may need to break it down into smaller goals. Do you really want a Ferrari, or will a reliable Toyota do the trick? Do you really want a house or will a really nice apartment suit your needs? When you're specific and realistic about your goals, the path to them materializes in front of you.

My first financial goal was to get rid of my outstanding debt. I wasn't thinking about retiring or living the lush life. I wanted to make more money so I could pay back what I owed. After my debt problem was solved, I tried to think of how much money I wanted.

I want to be a millionaire, was my first thought. But why? What I really wanted was to be able to retire at some point and live off my earnings. Being a millionaire was way too abstract an idea for me to accomplish. I'm fine with working until I'm sixty-five, but I'm quitting that day and retiring with what I have.

Then I saw that I didn't have to make a lot of money quickly, but I needed a better job that would help me attain these goals. I didn't have to make the money in two years. I still had thirty years from the time I set the goal. So I knew that in a job I would need to make enough to save at least 10 percent per year in a 401(k) or an IRA.

At the beginning of 2007, I wasn't close to these goals. I was working in a job I liked that didn't pay me much more than I needed to get by. I kept my head up and looked for other work. If I couldn't find a better job, I'd find an additional one.

Two jobs came my way. One was a well-paying freelance job that lasted for two weeks, and the other was a minimum-wage job working at a comedy club. Between the two of these extra jobs, I managed to save $4,000. It wasn't much, but it was better than I had done since the '90s. My confidence and self-worth increased, and out of nowhere, I got a job interview and nailed it. I dumped that money into an IRA.

How much control we have over our financial future is debatable. I can control how much I save and put away. I can't control what the economy will be like in 2034, when I plan to retire; what if I do have a million dollars and that's how much my monthly rent is? Maybe I'll get hit by a bus the day before and think I should've blown all the money. I can control what portion I save, but how much it will be worth when I retrieve it is not in my control.

Finding Your Inner A-Team

In 1972 a crack commando unit was sent to prison by a military court for a crime they didn't commit. These men promptly escaped from a maximum security stockade to the Los Angeles underground. Today, still wanted by the government, they survive as soldiers of fortune. If you have a problem, if no one else can help, and if you can find them, maybe you can hire the A-Team.
—From the show's opening

The A-Team was one of the best "And They Solve Crimes, Too" shows on television in the '80s. There were any number of these programs on then, within all kinds of parameters. A Guy Has a Super-Intelligent Car That Talks, A Trucker Has a Pet Monkey, A Guy Leads a Team of Stuntmen, and all of them solve crimes. But creator Stephen J. Cannell hit some sociological genius with *The A-Team.*

Every plot in the series was full of holes, but the lessons learned were solid. The team, supposedly in hiding, drove around in a very distinctive customized van. Murdock routinely escaped from various institutions but was never so insane as to jeopardize a mission. And, most unbelievably, for the thousands of rounds they fired, they never hit a single person. But what we have to learn from them will help us socialize with the Normies.

Interacting with the Normies is a difficult part of sobriety.

Interacting with the Normies is a difficult part of sobriety. If we'd gotten along with them in the first place, we probably wouldn't have started using in the first place. Since you didn't learn how to deal with them the first time, you'll have to learn to deal with them now.

Normies, at first viewing, seem like strange creatures. They leave beers unfinished. They open a bottle of scotch, have a drink, and don't drink from the same bottle again for months. They can keep a stash of wine in the cellar. They don't drink if they're about to drive or operate heavy machinery. They take the prescribed dosage on the side of the bottle instead of the whole bottle at once. Weird, huh? But wait, it gets weirder and weirder.

Normies socialize sober. They go out on dates, to dinner parties, celebrate holidays without ever taking a drink or smoking pot. Many of them don't drink unless they're at a wedding, and they only go to weddings they're invited to. I know, it sounds like an urban legend, like the story about the old lady who tried to dry off her poodle in the microwave, but it's totally true.

> **The first thing I suggest you do is diagnose your weak points, and then desensitize yourself to your fears.**

I hesitate to say our personalities are incomplete; rather, I'd say they're underdeveloped. You have all the tools you need to get by inside of you, but some of them are in a frozen state, like when Darth Vader froze Han Solo in carbonite. Your ability to go out on a date sober was frozen since the age of fifteen, when you went on your first date by getting plowed on two wine coolers first. Instead of developing those social skill sets, you were getting drunk or high. But there is still time to develop said skills.

I won't underplay this. It's going to be scary. But really, if you think of all the scary things you've been through over the years that would make the average Normie crap his pants, you'll see that you're a brave one. You've been in bad drug deals, been abandoned while passed out; some of you have flatlined in the back of ambulances. If you've been legally dead ever in your life and come back, you're tough enough to learn how to hang out with a group of strangers.

The first thing I suggest you do is diagnose your weak points, and then desensitize yourself to your fears. People with phobias are often made to confront their fears gradually, by slowly getting higher on a ladder, rung by rung, over a period of months, or by meeting a series of progressively larger dogs, or by hiring hookers that dress like nuns. The best way to diagnose your personality type is by using the A-team.

Hannibal

Hannibal is the planner of the team. He's a master of disguise, rarely spotted by his enemies whilst walking among them.

If you're a Hannibal, your life is orderly. You know where everything is. You don't lose important items. You make appointments and keep them, never showing up late. You can't stand indecisiveness on a group level. Your polar opposite is Murdock.

As an Addict

You were the one who kept the scale and weighed everything out perfectly. When it was time for a beer run, you designated what would be purchased and collected the money from everyone. You rarely ran dry. You were an overachieving alcoholic, showing up first to work, often in a managerial position, and leaving last.

As a Recovering Addict

You're going to be happiest with service work. You need to run meetings, have sponsees, and be a part of organizational activities. It irritates you when you see meetings being run in an inefficient manner. Step work makes sense to you, but you like to break each step down into twelve more steps, and add other steps that were left out.

Pros

Hannibal's organizational skills are of good use. Paperwork, forms, and responsibility come naturally to the Hannibal. Less likely to relapse if kept busy. Confident, assertive, and enthusiastic.

Cons

You have a hard time taking direction. Asking for help is your biggest problem. You think your way is best, and it's hard for you to conceive otherwise. Idleness is unbearable. Stubborn.

B.A.

B.A. is the muscle of the outfit. When it's time to duke it out, this is the man who's called on. He's also the driver and mechanic. However, B.A. has a debilitating fear of flying.

If you're a B.A., people are intimidated by you. You usually get your way, without an argument. Earlier in life, you were likely tormented by a parent, sibling, or neighborhood bully, but once you surpassed that, no one would dare cross you. Your polar opposite is Face.

As an Addict

No one dared burn you in a drug deal, although some of them were afraid you were a cop. You were a bouncer or doorman, and broke up many more fights than you've ever been in. You've made bongs out of everything but other bongs. Some of those bongs had mechanical parts.

As a Recovering Addict

It's hard for you to find a sponsor who will be straight with you. You need to be pushed, but many people are afraid of your demeanor. When you find your right sponsor, your progress will be rapid. You have a hard time in job interviews, mostly because you scare the person interviewing you.

Pros

When there's something you want, you go directly after it. There's no hesitation or pussyfooting around. Your goals, once realized, are targeted and achieved.

Cons

Fear, ironically enough. While few things will scare a B.A., what does scare you completely dominates you in the situation. Your strength is thus rendered helpless. Has trouble with intimacy. Refuses to back down in situations even when it would greatly benefit you to do so.

Murdock

Murdock was the pilot of the bunch. On the show, he served as comic relief as the Hilarious Post-Traumatic Stress Disorder Guy. Aren't shell-shocked vets *hilarious*?

Murdock is the prankster, the artist, the performer, and the jester. Everyone loves having you in the group. Your polar opposite is Hannibal.

As an Addict

You did copious amounts of drugs that were given to you by those who loved having you around. You were the "fun" drunk. You likely had a nickname that people shouted when you entered the bar. Though you angered many people who were the brunt of your pranks, you escaped without a scratch.

As a Recovering Addict

Chaos still rules. You have poor organizational skills, are late often, and lose important items. A creative outlet is imperative for your sobriety, but you may have a hard time acquiring the necessary items, bookings, or gallery space in which to showcase your talents. People think the stories of your bottom moments are hilarious.

Pros
There's always room for Murdock. Social groups accept you quickly. You have enormous amounts of creative and artistic talent. People love to hear you talk in meetings.

Cons
Are rarely taken seriously as a person with wants and needs. As a heterosexual man, women often want you around but just as a friend. It's hard for you to find a job, even though your friends love having you around.

Face
Face is the charmer. He was the one who talked the A-team in and out of any situation. No matter the situation, how high security it was, Face always found his way through locked doors and restricted access areas.

You can talk anyone out of anything, and you always get your way in the end. You get jobs based on the strength of your interview, whether or not you said you were qualified. Your polar opposite is B.A.

As an Addict
You were never arrested. Stopped by the police, yes, but always managed not to go downtown. Dealers fronted you drugs, even when they didn't want to; somehow you convinced them.

As a Recovering Addict

When told what to do by a sponsor, you may not be able to resist bargaining for something else. You'll be able to reenter society, as people treat you as a hero for kicking your addictions.

Pros

Despite your checkered past, people trust Face when you asks for responsibility, loans, or gifts. You're the first one to get a second chance.

Cons

Acquiring positions in life and material items, Face is never satisfied. You can't enjoy them; you only enjoy talking people into giving them up. There are never enough toys or joys for Face. Finding emotional value in life is difficult. You may find yourself in a position in which you do not have the skills to succeed and must further talk your way out of a situation.

Yo, dude, all this is great, but how the hell am I supposed to use this knowledge?

You see, you're supposed to have aspects of all four of these characters to be a complete person. Without your Hannibal, you'll never be able to get things done. Without your B.A., you'll be walked on by others and not be able to improvise in difficult situations. Without your Murdock, you'll never be able to live in the moment and truly enjoy life. Without your Face, you'll have trouble getting people to trust you.

Figure out which area is weak, and make that team member exercise. Start small.

If your Hannibal is weak, make paying your bills and being on time your priority. Clean your room; it needs it. Even if it's cleaner than it was when you were a junkie, it's not clean

> **As an addict, there was so much socialization done around drugs and alcohol, it'll be good for you to relearn how to talk about normal things. Be patient.**

enough. Just because there are no trash cans filled with puke doesn't mean it's clean.

If your Murdock is weak, take up a creative endeavor. Play an instrument or start a journal. You don't have to make it public; you don't need to go so far as to do a poetry reading or sign up for open mike night with all the Dylan wannabes. There's a real danger of thinking, "Because It Happened to Me, It's Interesting." Many artists fall into this trap, and write boring memoirs and screenplays.

If your B.A. is weak, you need to work on your physical body. Whether it's yoga, martial arts, or weightlifting, you'll get more in touch with your physical assertiveness. It's very common to gain a lot of weight in sobriety. This weight gain, especially after years of drug-induced skinniness, can lead to an inferior self-image. Getting in shape will positively affect how you see yourself, and thus, how the world around you sees you.

If your Face is weak, be more social. Make a new friend. Reunite with an old one. As an addict, there was so much socialization done around drugs and alcohol, it'll be good for you to relearn how to talk about normal things. Be patient. Some of your friends will rattle on incessantly about how brilliant their kid is even if he can't use a toilet, or about how expensive owning a house can be. Remember the stoner who, every single time he got high, talked about a particularly good bag of pot he bought ten years before?

Achieving Your Goals the Lee Marvin Way

Point Blank is one of my favorite Lee Marvin movies. It's hard to choose between his role as the biker in *The Wild One* or in the weird midwestern mafia flick *Prime Cut* or any of his other fine films. But one that sticks out to me is *Point Blank*.

In this film, Lee Marvin is after $93,000 that was his share of some unspecified heist. What stood out for me was his use of a step method to get his money back. He calmly yet violently moved from one step to the next in the quest to retrieve the money owed him.

We have two main lessons to learn from this: Be specific in your goal making, and be ardent with each step. Marvin doesn't look to get any more than a specific amount. He's not interested in getting $100,000, he wants what's coming to him. His resolve goes no further than what he needs to do for that part of his journey.

When I got sober, I wanted my life to improve. That's a very vague goal to have, so nonspecific that I may not notice or achieve satisfaction when it does happen. Think of your goals as a location where you want to be. Would you get in a car without knowing where you were going? Well, maybe. If you're reading this book, you likely have. But it didn't turn out well, did it? Would you try to drive to Boston from California by heading vaguely east without looking it up in an atlas or on a map? That's not a good idea, either. So I had to figure out exactly what I wanted for myself.

Getting sober is going to give you a lot of time that you used to spend staring at the TV in the bar. You have time to get most things in life done that you want to do. But first, you need to figure out what those things are.

I knew I needed more money. I was making around $10 an hour. That's not enough to live well on in San Francisco. I lived in substandard housing, in one of the tiniest apartments that I had ever lived in. My health was iffy at best, and I needed a better medical plan. Money won't buy you happiness, but poverty will make you want to kill yourself.

So how much did I want? The last time in my life that I had enough money to cover all my personal expenses I was making $40K per year. Unfortunately, instead of spending that at the dentist and putting money away in an IRA, I spent more than $15,000 that year on bars, cab rides, and Vegas trips; the rest of it, I wasted. The point is, $40K a year became my goal.

No one would give me that kind of money in the job market at the time. Those days were past. I needed to get some new skills or qualifications in order to get the job I wanted. I needed either more training or more education.

What would Lee Marvin do? When he needed his $93,000, he had nothing but one address of one person who was slightly involved in the old caper. He went from there, step by step, to figure out what he needed to do.

One of the job requirements I couldn't fulfill was a BA from a university. I had dropped out of college my senior year, many years before, with the idea that I would go back, but I never did. I either had time or money but never both. If people wanted to buy bad excuses and shitty reasons, I could've started a superstore. There was always something keeping me from going back, and most of it came down to that when I got off work, I wanted to drink all night. The most embarrassing part of this is that I had dropped out my senior year. I had less than a year to go.

Every other option I explored would take more than a year to complete. Various apprenticeships and training programs took longer than a year. The quickest action I could take to improving my job outlook was finishing school.

San Francisco State was the school that would graduate me the quickest. I had a lot of resentments about my previous time there, and with various faculty members from my department who were still there. I had to get over these problems. I had been carrying around grudges from ten-year-old incidents, and they were hindering me from achieving my goals. Drunk Me would've not gone back because of those resentments, but this was Sober Me who was trying to get into school.

Getting back in was a mess. On the university website, there were forms for new students and transfer students, but none for drunk students who dropped out in 1992 and wanted to go back twelve years later. I knew they would want transcripts from the previous schools, records I didn't have, but I couldn't let anything stop me.

I decided I would take getting back into school one day at a time, just as they say to take sobriety when you're a newcomer to recovery. I didn't have to get back into school with one click of an Internet button; I would be able to get in over a period of days, months, or years, whatever it took, but I resolved to do something for this quest every day.

My daily tasks ranged from short phone calls to long forms. Every day, I had a number to call to get a transcript, to set up an appointment with a guidance counselor, or to go down to San Francisco State in person to stand in a line for an hour. Since I had started school in the '80s, my records had not been kept on computers; they were kept on what was called microfiche, the high-tech version of microfilm. I was lucky that the people at all three of my schools were able to find them. I pictured them in some warehouse, akin to the closing scene of *Raiders of the Lost Ark,* where my college files were located right next to the ark of the covenant. Usually I spent five to fifteen minutes a day working on my plan.

One day, I was in. I received an email confirmation that said I had successfully reentered SF State. I was so excited, I forgot for a minute that I was only *in,* and I hadn't yet taken any of the classes. Getting in was only the beginning.

I looked online at the graduation requirements and saw that the program had radically changed since I'd been away. I had no idea which classes to take. Again, I felt like giving up, but I rallied up my inner Lee Marvin and set to the task of figuring out which classes to take.

I had only started on the journey. Once I figured out what I had to take, I had to go to the classes. Once I was in the classes, I had to do all the work and show up to all the lectures. Once I was done with the classes, I had to take the remaining classes. I soon saw it was a long process that would take me two years to work my way through.

There were sacrifices that were made. I couldn't be in plays, which I had come to enjoy but which required a lot of rehearsal time. I had to cut my work hours to go to the classes that met at the most inconvenient times. I lived in the smallest room I'd ever lived in so I could afford to cut my work hours and still be able to eat.

There was one English lit class I had to take that freaked me out when I saw the syllabus. There was twice as much reading on there than I had thought there would be. There were also lots of critical essays to turn in. Writing papers for lit courses is no joke. There's no room for bullshitting the way through. It's definitely one of those fields in which one has to know the subject matter to pass. I didn't see any way that I could do that much work. But I realized, in this class as well as in life, that I only had to do the work that is required of me each week, not all of it at once. One day at a time. Take it in steps.

That's when it really hit me what this step thing is all about. 12 Step is not some kind of random ritual to put us through; it helps us build life skills that get us through each day. It's not only about quitting drugs and drinking, it's about living without them, really living our lives without escapes and crutches and false security mechanisms.

> **12 Step is not some kind of random ritual to put us through; it helps us build life skills that get us through each day.**

Eventually, I was done. I received a diploma in the mail, with the automated signature of Arnold Schwarzenegger. I had done at the age of thirty-five what many twenty-two-year-olds had done. Graduating with a BA from a state school would be a step down for a lot of people I knew, but for me it was huge.

Being Happy

Maybe you don't know what goals you want to accomplish. You may have spent the recent parts of your life simply getting by day to day and working around your addiction. Take the obsession to use away, and there's a big hole to fill in its place. The best place to start is with a simple question: What makes you happy?

Aside from drug, alcohol, and sexual experiences, what were the last times that you were happy? Where were you? What were you doing? Who were you with? If you can find a pattern in all of these moments, you may find there's something you truly enjoy.

I'm not saying that you have to do what makes you happy for a living. Maybe the opposite; many people find that a fun atmosphere is ruined by having to work in it. My favorite jobs were minimum wage jobs; if I had to do something I loved for a career, I'd probably work in a used bookstore or in a movie theater. Those jobs won't service me through old age.

But you should find something that makes you happy, even as a hobby or a side interest. You'll need an activity that you enjoy, whether it's sports, video games, or playing music. It may have been a while since this one thing wasn't getting high, but it will be in your memory somewhere.

Your goals should include these activities in your life. It's not wise only to work, with no personal reward. You only get one life, and you should enjoy it. But rather than morally and physically destructive activities, now you need to find constructive and spiritually rewarding ways to occupy your time.

Taking Good Care of Your Hustle Monkey

Doctors and medical professionals will tell you that underneath your skin you are full of bones, blood, and vital organs. While this may or may not be true, there are other important items of interest inside you. You are full of monkeys.

You're likely familiar with the Gambling Monkey, Liquor Monkey, Drug Monkey, and Hump Monkey. These monkeys are the little imps that get you into trouble when you're trying to behave yourself. Like when you try to make it a day without incident, and soon enough, you're down at the bar, betting on the game, drinking whiskey, and after last call, you're going home with someone you just met and doing lines with them. It's the monkeys that do it to you. While you're likely in at least one 12-Step group to deal with these monkeys, there's one monkey that you need to cage maybe more than the others: the Hustle Monkey.

The Hustle Monkey is the most insidious of all your inner primates. It's the one most responsible for your relapses, unless, of course, you have the rare Relapse Monkey.

The Hustle Monkey is the most insidious of all your inner primates. It's the one most people don't know about, yet it's the one who is most responsible for your relapses, unless, of course, you have the rare Relapse Monkey. If you have a Relapse Monkey, you'll need to be in an inpatient program or the heiress to a hotel magnate. But most of us need to watch out for Hustle Monkey.

Hustle Monkey likes the act of *acquiring* our vices, more so than our respective vice monkeys like their vices. Hustle Monkey is the one who gets you to hit the liquor store at one minute before close. Hustle Monkey likes stealing and selling CDs for dope money. Hustle Monkey likes to buy a whole ounce of weed with the idea that you'll sell enough to get three-eighths for free. Hustle Monkey is the most morally debilitating of all of them. It likes to steal, scam, and otherwise procure the vices and their tools.

What Does a Good Hustle Monkey Do?

Every successful self-made person has a Hustle Monkey. It's not just limited to those with addictions. The problem is, in addicts it's learned to use its hustle powers for mischief rather than productivity. Don't blame it, though; after all, it's just a monkey. What does it know?

Richard Branson, the founder of Virgin, started the brand with a mail-order record business in 1970. Thirty-seven years later, he's starting the first orbital space travel passenger airline. Branson's Hustle Monkey is the size of King Kong.

The Hustle Monkey need not be that big. Smaller monkeys have inspired people with different dreams to do taxidermy at home, open bait shops, and get MFAs. But it's not how big your Hustle Monkey is, it's how you get your Hustle Monkey to work for you.

Nothing worth having in life comes easy. If you're reading this, you're probably thinking of something like heroin or a stripper's phone number. But if you apply those same principles to other more positive ideas, you can retrain your Hustle Monkey to work for you.

Think of everything other people have that looks like a pain in the ass to get: houses, jobs, monogamous spouses. People have to work for those things. It's the way our American culture works: the only incentive for breaking your back and depleting your psyche every day is so you can have the necessities of life. Some people think you should be given everything you need to live. We call them socialists. If America's founders thought this way, they would've said somewhere that we have a right to life, liberty, and the pursuit of happiness. If this was important to them, they would've written it down somewhere, in pen . . . . Oh wait, they did. But this isn't about politics, it's about you. You, too, can have all these things.

Think of what you went through to score dope with no money, to shoot up with no rig and only a plastic spoon in sight, and to get out of the house while wearing the ankle monitor. To normal people, this would seem like a world of trouble. They wouldn't know the first thing about any of this. To us, it seems like the normal ins and outs of everyday life. What I'm trying to get across to you is this idea: What is one man's short con is another man's thesis paper.

Think of some simple scam, like Brick In A Box. First, you have to find an empty box that used to contain something like a camcorder that you could resell; how many times have you looked to only find boxes for Pop-Tarts and tampons? Then, you have to find a brick, of course, never around when you need one. Then you have to find some mark who's dumb enough to buy it without looking inside. Sure, it works, but it takes up a lot of time and trouble, all for $20. You likely would've made more than that working for minimum wage. But that fact never stopped you. You had that incentive of scoring dope at the end of it all, but it's the Hustle Monkey inside you that kept you in the moment of one step to the next in the face of being dopesick.

These are the same qualities your Hustle Monkey can use to get you through the more legitimate areas of your life. If you can have this same approach to hunting for one job after another, and interviewing fearlessly, you will get the job you want. If you hunt for the right fixer-upper, and are willing to restore it to livable conditions, you will get the house you want. If you can focus on making your partner happy, in the face of temptation and live selflessly, you can maintain a monogamous relationship.

And no, you're not getting a new monkey. You're keeping the same old one. You're still an alcoholic, a drug addict, or whatever the case may be. Retraining the Hustle Monkey takes overt effort, and a strength of will that makes your obsessive cravings for drugs look like a weekend hobby. But first things first. You need to come up with some goals for yourself. Before you send the Hustle Monkey to work, you need to find out what you want from life.

Chapter 7

The Artist
and Recovery

Get Up

There are plenty of artists in recovery. Furthermore, there are many famous artists who have never been in recovery, but are deep in addiction. I've often talked about what makes this happen. Does getting high help creativity?

My best answer to questions like this one is that what makes us good artists is also what makes us prone to being good addicts. We don't pay attention to the status quo. We maintain a perspective outside of the normal world. We often have childhood trauma. We thrive in situations that would frighten most people.

What is an artist? That's a self-determining definition, much like admitting that you are an addict. It has to do with how you view yourself and where your passions lie; people can have artistic talent without being artists, and you better believe there are plenty of artists out there without artistic talent.

I count all creative types as artists: musicians, comedians, poets, and whoever else works in self-expressive media. While some of us think in sound, others in visuals, and others in words; we all seem to come back to having at our core this ball of creativity. Accessing that creative center is the first part of the artistic process. Taking the message to the outside world is the second part of that process.

The Artist, the Hot Stove Toucher

There's a lengthy correlation between brilliant artists and drug use. All of my artistic heroes were addicts of some kind at varying levels. The drugs and alcohol that are consumed change, but the addiction never does. Arthur Rimbaud, Edgar Allan Poe, Charles Baudelaire, Charles Bukowski, Hunter S. Thompson, William S. Burroughs, Jim Carroll, Philip K. Dick. Those are just the writers. If I had to get into the filmmakers, musicians, actors, and painters, I'd need another book for all of them. They relate their productivity to drug use, and say it helped, but did it really?

Most people who touch a hot stove will immediately learn not to touch it, but other personalities will touch it more.

The same qualities that make a person a great artist also make him or her a likely addict. This personality takes no rules as a given truth, and looks at the world from a fresh perspective. This personality type I like to call The Hot Stove Toucher.

Most people who touch a hot stove will immediately learn not to touch it, but other personalities will touch it more. How long can I stand to touch it? What does burning feel like? Boy, it feels good when I stop touching it. What does burning finger smell like? What if I try the other hand?

Applied to the art world, this personality innovates new usage of technique and content. The painter uses color and form in a new way. The filmmaker shoots from new angles. The writer explores new narrative styles. Most of the creative types we studied in college broke or bent rules in spite of popular opinion, and often to the point of career destruction.

Applied to drugs, this personality immediately damages itself. Crack is addictive? Give me some. This could kill me, but what if I take just enough so it won't, and how much is just enough? Give me some. If I drink too much of this, I'll puke? Give me some. Furthermore, it doesn't learn but tries again: this time I won't drink so much, this time I won't mix the two drugs, this time I won't shoot it I'll just smoke it. This personality thrives on danger and risk.

As a child, I always heard plenty of warnings about drugs and alcohol. Every year in school, some guy came around for drug and alcohol awareness week telling his tales of getting loaded and becoming an addict. A similar guy came around every year to church youth rallies. There was a whole industry of guys who used to be drug addicts but now talked to kids. The problem is, I never really listened to the full message, only what I wanted to hear.

What I heard was, "Go this far and no further," rather than "Don't go there at all." The guys' lives always sounded pretty cool in the beginning, while they were a KISS roadie, a Miami disco king, or the leader of a biker gang. In the middle of the story is When I Went Too Far, and someone dies or gets maimed and the guy goes to jail for it, where he finds Jesus, then gets out and comes and talks to us. Inadvertently, they always sold the lifestyle. They always talked about awesome hot rods, money, and girls. The only thing that stopped me at this point was the idea that God didn't like it when I got high or did drugs, but when I lost my faith, there was no God to be upset.

With no God to anger, I was free to pursue all those crazy stories I'd heard over the years. I was definitely getting drunk, and a hit of acid was in my future, and there are going to be some awesome concerts, and I will get laid all the time. I'd heard all the cautionary tales, but I had learned from them that you stop right before you go too far and you're okay.

The only lessons I learned from my own mistakes were the wrong ones. If I drank too much one night and got sick,

I'd blame that I didn't eat enough beforehand or that I mixed two kinds of alcohol. If I got into a fight, it was because I was at the wrong bar. If I fell asleep on the train and ended up several counties away from where I wanted to go, I swore that the next time, I'd stand up the whole way. The idea that I shouldn't drink that much never occurred as the proper solution. Normal people got sick off a type of liquor and never drank it again; I'd merely mix it with something different.

Here's to Irony, one of my Higher Powers, that in some way I'm now one of those guys I never listened to. Instead of getting high to see Ted Nugent, I was watching The Melvins. Change the names of a few things, but the story is overall the same. If I went back to my old church and told them stories, I'm sure I'd have the same effect on them as the old druggies had on me.

I've known a lot of artists who thought that doing the drugs of their heroes would help them attain the talent of said heroes. It's a common fallacy that somehow perpetuates in the art world. Whether it's Jimi Hendrix and acid, Bukowski and booze, or William S. Burroughs and heroin, it's fairly common for young artists to experiment this way.

My Life in the Art Scene

When I was eighteen, I found the world of spoken word poetry. It was 1987. I thought it was fun, and liked to participate in it when I could. The next year I read a Charles Bukowski poem for the first time and decided immediately to pursue a career in poetry.

I dropped all other artistic aspirations from my life. I was taking classes for visual arts and had been planning on entering film school at some point. I easily stopped trying to sing for a punk band, which wasn't hard since none of the band members wanted me anyway. All that remained was poetry.

The more subculture writing I read, the more I found drugs and alcohol. Since I was drinking on a regular basis and doing cocaine, acid, and mushrooms whenever opportunity arose, this made perfect sense to me. I was going to be the next William S. Burroughs, Philip K. Dick, Hunter S. Thompson, or Charles Bukowski. It made perfect sense to me to devote the majority of my free time to writing and getting wasted.

I moved to San Francisco looking for its famous poetry scene, and I found it quickly. I also found that like my heroes and myself, the SF poetry scene was rife with drugs and alcohol. I was still underage, but most of the bars I was going to for readings didn't seem to care.

Soon I was doing shows at places like The DNA lounge. As I was not yet twenty-one, they made me wait outside with Fritz the Doorman until it was time for me to go on. When I was announced, I'd run inside, do my time on stage, run backstage and slam a drink or snort a line of speed, then leave the club and go home.

There was also a burgeoning South of Market warehouse scene going at the time, spaces legal to live in after the live/work laws were passed. Many of the places had weird little shows with a lot of odd performance art. The spaces were literally people's homes the rest of the time, and sometimes S/M dungeons as well.

The poets were from the marginal parts of society. They were sex workers, mentally challenged, and nonclassifiable freaks and fuckups. It was the first time in my life I felt normal. No matter how misfit I felt before, these people were way beyond any level that I was. Better than that, they loved my backstory. When they found out I had been in a cult and was more or less a failed preacher, I got credibility in the art scene. It was like they were jealous of my trauma. The very things I was ashamed of and afraid to tell people about were what made me cool.

I started running my own shows. Throughout the '90s, I put on more than three hundred events. I attracted the worst fuckups of the entire Bay Area poetry scene. Together, we built our own mini-scene of debaucherous poetry. Poets shot up in the bathroom before they went onstage. Drinking wasn't normal; being completely blitzed was. They'd show up already destroyed from the El Rio's dollar-well-drink Monday happy hour.

All the while, I was putting together a body of work that I hoped would be a book someday. There were short stories, comics, and poetry. I was slowly getting pieces published in underground magazines and growing a reputation. Then Manic D Press, which had published a few chapbooks for me, told me they wanted to put together a full-length collection of my work.

I thought that when the book came out, it would change my life. The book would become its own phenomena and would have a dedicated readership. There would be movies made from the stories, and I would get rich from options and rights. None of that happened. The book died on the shelf. It barely got reviews. One review, in the *Austin Chronicle*, trashed it. I wasn't ready for negative attention.

As other friends and Bay Area writers changed from being hopefuls to being authors, I wasn't emotionally equipped to deal with their success. Every time the *Bay Guardian* or the *SF Weekly* or the *San Francisco Chronicle* wrote a good review of someone else's book, it was reinforcement that they didn't like mine.

As time went on, my resentments grew more quickly and to a higher level. I was sure I was being shut out of the local media by some conspiratorial plan; I had angered the wrong person, either with my scintillating talent or with my tell-it-like-it-is attitude. At that point, any new author who got a good review became One Of Them.

In the late '90s, the poetry scene as I knew it was gone. Street poet stalwarts such as Jack Micheline and David Lerner had died. Diet Popstitute, emcee of the Klubstitute performance art night, also had died. Dozens more were too strung out to participate anymore. Most people, though, just quit. They went to the suburbs and had kids or got workaholic jobs; it was definitely a better life for most of them, but it eliminated a majority of the dependable artists in the scene. What came in their place was worse than I could imagine.

The movie *Slam* came out on video, and young kids everywhere wanted to be Saul Williams. This wasn't what caused the downfall of San Francisco poetry, but it was the defining metaphor. San Francisco street poetics never recovered.

What had been the voice of the Mission poets was replaced with the hip-hop poetic of the East Coast. Just as the neighborhood was quickly changing face and population, so was its art. The black-clad subcultural artist types were forced out by the graphic designers and dot-commers flooding in. Rents rose, bars went from punk to house music, and the price of burritos went up two dollars.

Hip-hop came from street poetry, but you shouldn't take street poetry from hip-hop. You should take it from the street, direct from the source. Street poetry should sound like your neighborhood, not something from a video or a movie. More poets in the hip-hop scene steal from Gil Scott Heron than know who he is. The man has been stolen from so much no one knows who the work belonged to in the first place. There are still kids out there working with a many-generation version of Miguel Piñero's delivery style.

All of this, I took very personally. The Bay's natural influx of transients brought in a lot of kids with MFAs who were amazing performers. But their writing left a lot to be desired. No one who came to the scene after around 1997 or so made any significant literary contributions. Performance-wise, though, they made me obsolete.

For years, people wanted the Iggy Pop style of performance; they wanted us to get wasted and scream our poems into mikes. We never performed straight. I often had drinks brought to the edge of the stage when I performed. We brought new poems to the stage each week or we were heckled. The new scene was about memorizing a few poems and executing them with precision. I was outdated and done.

Charles Ellik gave me a feature spot at his venue, The Starry Plough. It's a long-running slam venue, one of the best known in the country. It was my chance to show everyone from the local slam community what I could do with twenty minutes.

All day long, the day of the show, I tried not to get too fucked up to go on. I knew I could still get as wasted as I wanted afterward, but I had to maintain at least a little beforehand. By this time, I was drinking two pints of whiskey a day: the morning pint and the evening pint.

I thought I could cut back to a half-pint before the show. That would be enough to kill the shakes, I thought, to get me right so I could go on. But the half-pint was a tease. I drank the rest of the pint shortly thereafter.

I went to the show. The Plough was a beer-only joint. No whiskey. I got a beer, but it didn't go down well. Drinking beer for me by then was like smoking an ultralight cigarette. I found out I wouldn't be going on for a while, and I decided to go to the store.

I bought a half-pint of whiskey and a Coke. I drank them quickly outside the club. When I went back in, I was feeling just right. I ordered a pitcher of beer and waited to go up.

When Charles called my name, I stood up and knew I was fucked. Even though the beer didn't feel like much going down, the combination of that with the whiskey had me destroyed. I made it to the stage, but I wasn't going to do much with it. I was so drunk, I couldn't read my own poems off a piece of paper. So much for the poetic genius I thought I was.

I made it to the stage, but I wasn't going to do much with it. I was so drunk, I couldn't read my own poems off a piece of paper.

Since the late '80s, I had always been good at poetry. I knew I was a fuckup in a lot of other arenas, but I felt like I had something special when it came to poetry. I had finally lost the one thing that mattered to me.

I had gone from being a hard-drinking poet to a drunk who used to write. I had created a self-image of a bourbon-drinking street poet, the little Bukowski. It was all bullshit. I was a drunk with a book that no one gave a shit about.

That night I thought about my dead heroes.

Bukowski died in his seventies; there was no way I was making it that far. When he was thirty-five he woke up in LA

> **Part of me wanted to stop, but my fears were bigger than that part. These fears turned out to be illusions; they were not attached to any real threats.**

County Hospital. It took him ten years to drink himself there. They told him if he drank again, he'd die. But as I saw it, Bukowski was better off at fifty than I was at thirty-two. Somehow he was able to handle his shit better. He wrote twenty or thirty poems a week by his own estimation. I was barely writing ten poems a year.

Bill Hicks died a month before Bukowski had, but at a much younger age. Hicks died of pancreatic cancer at the age of thirty-two. But by then, he'd left behind hours of recorded brilliance. I looked at my one book. It was nothing compared to what he'd done. We were the same age.

Then there were the dozens of actors and comedians who weren't heroes but died too young from drugs, alcohol, and chaos. John Belushi. Chris Farley. Sam Kinison. When I was in junior high school, and heard that John Belushi had died, I thought thirty-three was a ripe old age. Thirty-three was right around the corner for me.

Even after all that, it took me another six months or so to get into a program and quit for good. I'd had another idea that had already washed out, that I would write a screenplay, sell it, and use the money to get into a treatment facility like Promises, where I would network and get a nice Hollywood job when I left. That didn't work out at all.

My Fears

Fear kept me from going to a 12-Step program. The last year I drank, I didn't enjoy it. Part of me wanted to stop, but my fears were bigger than that part. These fears turned out to be illusions; they were not attached to any real threats.

Fear #1: Once I quit, I wouldn't be able to write anymore

I wasn't really writing anymore anyway. There were a lot of pieces started, but few of them finished. It was never a question of talent, but always a matter of execution. Aside from the actual writing, there was no way I could get together a manuscript or make any kind of deadlines.

Fear #2: People would feel ripped off if I performed sober

I really thought that people wanted to see me wasted up on stage. I bought into that myth that performers were better when they were on drugs. But I had proven that I couldn't perform anymore while high or drunk.

Fear #3: I would lose my credibility as a street poet if I was sober

I considered 12-Step artists as sellouts. I really thought less of them as creative types. I'm sure I have lost some credibility now—with drunks. This fear took a few 12-Step meetings to get over. Other artists I respected took me to meetings where I quickly found out that a lot of writers I've known were now sober.

My fears were unfounded. Maybe they were legitimate to a point, but they didn't really hold up under pressure. When I faced them, there was nothing there.

The Art of the Grudge

What I saw later, while doing step work, changed me as an artist forever.

In Step 4, you're supposed to list all your resentments. Ever. It's a big task that a lot of people can't get past. I didmine by sections of my life. There was grade school, junior high, high school/Boston, high school/Arkansas, immediate family, other relatives, roommates of all eras, and several different churches. I wrote up a separate one just for my art life.

I had resentments against other writers, venues, journalists, editors, publications, and publishers. Writers who had success that I didn't. Venues that wouldn't book me. Journalists who wouldn't write about me, and specifically some who had but later cut me out of the articles. Editors, publications, and publishers who rejected my work while publishing other work I thought to be inferior.

I've seen drugs and alcohol, or the chaos that comes with them, destroy a lot of writers. I saw a whole other scene of performance artists decimated by HIV. But jealousy, envy, and bitterness that fuel resentment and grudges have destroyed more creative people's careers than AIDS, crack, and heroin combined.

My jealousy was at a debilitating level. I couldn't be friends with people because of it. While it's normal to be somewhat jealous of the success of others, I felt that if you got a good review in the *Chronicle,* you were no friend of mine.

The energy I was spending with these negative emotions was keeping me from creating new work. There's nothing worse in a poet than an inordinate amount of self-pity. The poems were bad. There's no other way to put it. While my early poems were genuine, once these defects of character took over, the poems read like parodies of bad poetry.

The Not So Secret of My Success

While my impetus for working the steps wasn't achieving publishing success, that's exactly what happened.

While other people in the program were praying and meditating to get closer to their Higher Powers, I was creating on a daily basis. The better I became as a writer, the closer I became to my Ideal Image.

> **It's not so much that drugs and alcohol will ruin your talent, but they will definitely ruin your execution.**

When I wasn't writing, I turned to editing. I had a lot of material from the previous five years that hadn't been edited or finished. They existed on computer files, written on scraps of paper, and drunkenly scrawled in journals. It's not so much that drugs and alcohol will ruin your talent, but they will definitely ruin your execution. There was nothing finished in the batch. Many of the pieces were the same poem written over and over, and yet not a complete poem ever.

I knew that to become my Ideal Image, I had to have a body of work published. I wanted ten books. That, to me, would be a significant accomplishment for one lifetime. Just as they said One Day At A Time in my 12-Step group, I decided One Book At A Time. Still, it seemed daunting. I hadn't had a book in the previous seven years. Most of my contacts in publishing were no longer working at the same companies. I wasn't sure how to start.

Sitting in a meeting, the solution became clear: I would get a new book in a series of steps. First, I'd write a new manuscript. Second, I'd edit it into a presentable format. Third, I'd find a list of publishers that might be interested. Fourth, I'd submit it as many times as required until it was accepted.

But it didn't end there. I'd make sure the book was successful if I was going to get more. Fifth, I'd work peacefully with my editor. Sixth, I'd promote the book once it came out.

Seventh, I'd really push the book once it came off the new titles rack and became yesterday's news. Eighth, I'd continually work on the next manuscript to have it ready for the next book.

One of my challenges was what to write. The manuscript I could have done the most quickly would be a poetry manuscript. The drawback to this is that poetry is the worst-selling form of writing out there and it also is one of the most difficult forms to get published in book format. Many publishers start with poetry, but as they evolve into bigger entities, they tend toward prose.

Such was the case with Manic D Press. When I approached the editor, she told me she didn't want to see a book of poetry, that I should write her a novel. I knew that my book of poems was a good one. I didn't want to leave them behind. The closest I was to a manuscript was a book of poems, not writing a novel from scratch.

I noticed that Gorsky Press made fine-looking books, but hadn't published anybody that I knew. Also, their distribution was not what it could be. But still, I could tell they were headed in the right direction. As the Alternative Press Expo was coming up soon, I would have a chance to meet with representatives of the publisher in person.

I met Sean Carswell, one of the two people behind Gorsky Press, at the APE show just as I thought I would. I asked him if he was looking at manuscripts. He told me that he only took new manuscripts through a contest.

Contests. Don't get me started. I don't like contests. The short of it is that most contests are a waste of time. I didn't want to be anywhere near it. I wanted to move on and find another publisher. But that was Old Me talking. New Me was up for playing by the rules, even if they sounded stupid. This is a prime example of how we, as artists, can turn our will over to a Higher Power, when that Higher Power is the artist we want to be.

My idea was that I'd play by the rules, lose the contest, and then convince Sean to publish my book anyway, as I could help him get better distribution through my contacts in the industry. I resolved that even if he didn't want to publish my book, I should help him anyway; it would be the right thing to do. Then the unexpected happened: I won first place in the contest, which was a cash prize and publication of what would be *Whiskey & Robots*.

I took the cash and paid for a semester's tuition at San Francisco State. In the past, money like that often led to a bad weekend in Reno. I quickly spent all but $18 of it at the university registrar, and bought dinner with the rest, which included a Coke (not just water) and a slice of cheesecake. Fancy!

Lies Artists Tell Ourselves

I had an obsession with failing that tied in directly to my drinking. I let the smallest obstacle turn into an unscalable wall of defeat. At the first rejection, I cursed the entire rest of the industry for not approving my art. I complained that no one wanted my work, but in reality, I had only shown it to a few people. All this misunderstanding and rejection from the world was a really good excuse to tie one on.

No one understands my work. Does anyone ever see your work? Do you have a manuscript or portfolio ready for submission? Are you self-sabotaging by making your work so inaccessible that no one in his right mind could ever understand it? Is there the slightest possibility that you need to improve? Tough questions, but ask them of yourself. Maybe the problem isn't with them, it's with your work.

The only ones who make it are ass kissers. What's an ass kisser? People who don't get wasted beyond recognition at literary events? People who follow submission guidelines? People who work hard, ignore rejection, and keep trying? I think you see where I'm going with this. The only ones who make it are hard workers.

The system is set up against me. Simply put, this is some paranoid bullshit. The system doesn't even know about you. You'd have to be a whole lot more important to deserve such a conspiracy. The system is extremely difficult for anyone to work through. Not just you, pal. It's tough for everyone trying to break in.

Self-Image and the Artist

I had this image of myself as this subcultural underground literary hero. I had been part of a really awesome street poetry scene that people still ask me about today. But as time went on, it was this image that dragged me around and ruled my life.

I pictured myself with a bottle of whiskey in one hand and a book of my poems in the other. I was a middle finger in the hand of American literature. I was the Iggy Pop to the Dan Fogelbergs of academia. I was a tough guy poet, a Bukowski with steel-toe Doc Martens.

One of the ways this image got me into trouble was how it promoted my drug and alcohol use. There were a lot of times that I rationalized extreme behavior as keeping with my extreme poetry lifestyle. Truth was, I wanted to do all of those drugs and drink all that booze. But I would convince myself it was to gain experience or perspective, in my quest to be the next Hunter S. Thompson or whomever.

Ironically, this image was what people didn't like about me and my work. There were plenty of instances when I wasn't asked to participate in a reading series or a festival because of my problematic drinking. It was never a question of my talent, it was the answer that everyone knew when they asked themselves how I would behave.

In 1995, I was asked to go to Birmingham Southern College for a writing festival. It was my first real university reading. I was given a plane ticket, a stipend, and my own hotel room. This was luxurious beyond my imagination. Beth Lisick, who was also going, was told by our publisher not to let me get too drunk. I was one of the best our publisher could send, but she had her doubts about the impression I would leave. I did get too drunk there, almost constantly. I wasn't too drunk to perform, as would happen years later at the Starry Plough. But at all the afterparties, I got hammered. I was already out there enough, with my Charles Manson hair and my Charles Bukowski tee shirt, but I had to go the full distance and slam the Jack Daniel's whiskey as well. The next year found Jeffrey McDaniel and Beth Lisick, my travel mates, both in *The Best American Poetry* from that year, included by someone who was at that festival. I didn't make it in the book, which was a real shock. Why not? I didn't understand. I still can't say for sure, but what I do know is that Beth and Jeffrey maintained themselves on a social level, whereas I frightened the literary horses. I didn't get a single booking from that festival.

Usually, now, when I go somewhere and do my best, I'll get one or two offers to go another place and perform as well, or I'll be asked to submit a piece for publication. My talent goes only so far. After that, it's how I treat other people. No one wants to work with a drunk. No one wants to take a chance on a possible problem.

As I could then, I'm sure you can think of plenty of artists who are troublesome addicts who still get gigs and chances to display work. But for every one of them, there are plenty more people who can't get a break because they're such social disasters. If you book an addict, you're opening yourself to having an act that shows up late or not at all. Working with anyone during the production process of something like a CD or a book is often emotionally draining; with an addict, it can be a nightmare.

There are a lot of artists out there. If you're at the top of your game, if you are at the level of Led Zeppelin or Richard Pryor, you will be booked and worked with regardless of how you act. But only a few artists and entertainers will ever achieve that level of success. After that top tier of name talent, there are a lot of people who are really good at what they do but are not household names. Unfortunately, there are only a few spots in every art form for these people to shine. If you're problematic, you're eliminating yourself from this list. Unless you're the person filling the room with ticket buyers, unless your name sells the book sight unseen, unless your name gets the song airplay, all you have is talent and behavior.

Humility and the Artist

Pride is an artist killer. Pride will take you out. Pride will fuck with you until you give in. With pride, you can justify resentment, jealousy, and envy. Pride will keep you from doing what is necessary to advance yourself, since you erroneously think those things are below you. As a defect of character, it's one you have to eradicate.

But this pride is only a tool of your addiction. Your addiction will use your sense of self to trick you into relapsing. You will rationalize usage in order to look good in front of others, even if you don't really want the drugs or booze.

There are artists who create and artists who complain. If you're doing one you're not doing the other. The complaining is a point of pride. With the energy you spend bitching about how someone didn't give you the gig you deserved, or about how somebody else undeservedly got a good review, you could be writing your next book or painting your next masterpiece. Pride keeps you from creating.

In the writing world, I've seen pride keep success from many writers. The prideful writer only wants to be in the most prestigious magazines and submit work to the most well-respected publishers. Meanwhile, the other writers are getting published.

Pride also keeps people from walking into a room and saying they want help. Pride is what keeps people from getting to Step 1. Pride doesn't want you to admit that you have a problem. Pride thinks that everyone else is the problem.

The only solution I see here is to switch the pride to other areas of your life, and to learn humility. This is a prime case in which a character attribute can be used for the good or ill of yourself. Pride isn't inherently bad; it's more like a trophy case.

> **Get over yourself. You're lying in a puddle of your own failure, imagining yourself to be some kind of misunderstood genius, reveling in the image that you're a Dylan Thomas or Edgar Allan Poe.**

Pride follows motivation. How you're using your pride is more important to look at than what you're proud of. Be proud of the car you restored, since it took determination and perseverance; not because it makes other people's cars look like junk. Be proud of getting yourself in shape, because it takes discipline in diet and exercise; not because you can use it to intimidate others. The key here is that you are doing these things for the satisfaction of the self, not for some external return. What's more frustrating than trying to impress other people and they don't give a shit?

If you're a failed artist and a successful addict, I'm guessing pride is your big problem. Get over yourself. You're lying in a puddle of your own failure, imagining yourself to be some kind of misunderstood genius, reveling in the image that you're a Dylan Thomas or Edgar Allan Poe.

The Tough Guy

Show me a tough guy, and I'll show you someone who was on the wrong end of a lot of childhood beatings. Whether from parents, siblings, or strangers, every tough guy I've met got his edge the hard way. Sure, there are some posers out there, but they're pretty easy to pick out. I'm talking about the guys who, regardless of size, are no one you'd ever fuck with.

The swagger, the tats, the clothes—all of it says *Don't fuck with me.* If you're a mixed martial arts–trained fighter, you can handle yourself in a fight, but if you're rocking 19-inch biceps, no one will dare start a fight with you. No one wants to start shit with a guy with a Fuck the World (FTW) tattoo across his forehead. Skinheads simply look more threatening than Emo Rockers. Most of all, it's the stare; a small man with a lot of fight in his eyes can often make much bigger men or several men back down. But the point is, the entire persona is there for preemptive self-defense.

Unfortunately, tied into the persona is drug and alcohol use. Whiskey drinking, speedball shooting, and the like are not within the realm of the wuss. It goes so far that IV-drug users will make fun of those who snort or smoke the same drugs. Asking a tough guy not to drink anymore is like telling him to trade his Indian motorcycle for a Ford Escort.

I met a man I'll call Harley in the program. I really looked up to this guy. His life sounded decidedly worse than mine; he had definitely bottomed out much worse than I had. I knew if he could get his shit together, so could I.

Harley was the archetypical bad boy. He had the rocka-billy look down. He had an awesome old car and a motor-cycle. He'd done real prison time. He'd kicked heroin. He was around 5 percent body fat and covered in tattoos. Best of all, his face and eyes showed that he had been somewhere ugly and made it back alive. But there was still something missing.

One day I heard the news that he had started drinking again. Not relapsing through some trauma or accident, he de-cided that he was cured of his addictions and decided to pick up the beer. After talking to him and to others, what I put together from everyone's conversation is that he thought not drinking was bad for his image.

When Harley was at Bondage a Go Go, the San Francisco club that caters to all kinds of fetishes, he often tried to pick up strippers on their night off or the Goth girls. He had some success, but not as much as his addict's sexuality craved. The one thing that betrayed his image was the soda water he sipped from. In fact, it creeped some of the women out that he would buy them drinks but not drink himself. So Harley made the decision that he would drink beer when out trying to pick up girls.

There were many opinions on this, but none of them were favorable. The wisest one was from another member of our group who told Harley to his face that he'd be shooting dope again inside six months. Harley denied it, but was shooting dope in five months. As far as I know, Harley's not put together much clean time since then.

Harley, while trying to impress a hooker he had brought home, shot a load of dope into his neck. This is something he'd done before with success, so it wasn't completely out of the question. The problem was that Harley hit his windpipe and blew out his vocal cords. He never talked above a whisper again.

The dope got the better of Harley's looks as well. His skin grayed into a pale mess. Something happened to his posture so that he could no longer stand up straight. His eyes lost their mystery; instead of looking like a man who'd been there and back, they looked like the eyes of an old dog who is begging you to shoot him and put him out of his misery.

In the end, Harley doesn't look like a tough guy. He looks like a junky. That's exactly what he is before he's anything else. He is the thing that shoots dope. That's the cruel trick of addiction. It will promise you something and take more than it gives.

I miss Harley quite a bit. He was an important person in my sobriety. The group he was a part of did more for me getting sober than the entire rest of the program combined. He shows up now and then, but can't put too much time together at a stretch.

All is not lost. I don't want to give the impression that I'm writing him off. But I do know that he went from having serious sober time to having tenuous sobriety. The road back is often more treacherous than the road there. Many more people have gotten sober once than have gotten sober twice.

Chapter 8

What I Learned from Joseph Campbell

There's a book that many people are required to read in college called *The Hero with a Thousand Faces*. It's written by a man named Joseph Campbell, who started a whole school of thought of comparative mythology. The easiest entry into his mind is through the DVD series called *The Power of Myth*. If you like what he has to say, check out *The Hero with a Thousand Faces*.

Hero, as I like to call it, is a standard textbook in many universities. That being said, it's also a really dry, dull read. Campbell's ideas were compelling, but the writing really isn't that interesting. If your reading skills or comprehension aren't that great, this may not be the book for you. But if you can power through *Hero*, you'll be well rewarded.

Campbell sought to find all of what he called "universal truths." He looked through thousands of years of mythology and religion seeking the similarities between them, the themes that run through the lives of humans then and now. For us to still suffer from the same pathos of a human who lived ten thousand years ago astounds me; we still have the same basic problems we've always had.

The Hero's Journey

Campbell also described what he called "the hero's journey." Much like he looked for the truths, Campbell found that heroes of all cultures seem to have similar life paths, with challenges and victories along the way. The concept has become a standard with Hollywood screenwriters, since George Lucas's endorsement of the book when discussing his *Star Wars* films. Often, what we are seeing as the clichéd plotlines of blockbuster cinema are millennia-old themes; these stories worked thousands of years ago, and they work now.

There's a lot to be learned by the atheist-addict from reading *Hero*. Seeking universal truths is a noble effort and will serve you well when taking moral inventories of yourself. Also, without banking on a set of dogmatic verbalism it shows different ways that humans have described victory and transformation.

Part One: The Departure

The Call to Adventure. This is the beginning of the story. The hero learns of a great danger, a threat to himself, his family, or his community. The hero must take action or all will be lost.

Read this as The Call to Sobriety. Your adventure doesn't start without sobriety. In fifteen years of drinking and writing, I wrote one book that didn't sell very well. In five years of sobriety, I've published two books and released a CD, as well as having a number of really nice gigs. More than anything, I wanted to be a writer. As I was living, it wasn't going to happen. That Moment of Clarity, as it's often called, is your calling to get sober.

I don't know what your personal adventure will be. Maybe it's a more grounded life than mine, maybe as a parent or as a better part of your family. You may be a successful businessperson hidden inside a drunk's body. For the artist, I can attest that once past a certain point of usage, the drinking and the drugs have to go away for you to be able to create.

Thinking of my life in this manner helped me understand that getting sober was the beginning of my story, not the end. I'm particularly miffed at the movies *Walk the Line* and *Ray,* as they both end with the protagonist getting clean. In both cases, the best parts of the artists' careers came after they quit drugs. Initially, when I got sober, I thought my life and fun were more or less over. It was just the opposite.

◇◇◇

Refusal of the Call. In this part of the journey, the hero declines the quest. The hero may not think himself qualified, or he has other things to do. He returns to his regular life, but things become much worse. His health, family, or community suffers, so he must begin his quest. Think of all the movies where the hero is coaxed out of retirement; he refuses, until his daughter is kidnapped, and then it's on!

> **Here are some of my favorite systems that never worked: only drink after 6 P.M., only drink one pint of whiskey per day, or only drink at home.**

The first time you know you should get clean and sober, you don't. Usually you put a "system" into place, such as switching to beer from whiskey, or only using after certain occasions. After a system fails, it's back to sick reasoning that it's not such a problem; I thought it was everyone else's Protestant ethics that made my drinking shameful.

If you have a system, you're an addict. If I told you I had a system for beating the horses, blackjack, or roulette, you'd tell me I was an idiot. Here are some of my favorite systems

The 12 Steps are your tools. Use them like a Magic 8 Ball, duct tape, or a Swiss Army knife.

that never worked: only drink after 6 P.M., only drink one pint of whiskey per day, or only drink at home. All of these worked worse for me than regular debauchery.

◇◇◇

Supernatural Aid. The hero is given tools and/or weapons with which to complete his quest. He may not understand their use or power, but somehow, with these items, he'll be victorious. The fun of a James Bond movie is in all the gadgets he has to accomplish his mission; it's not about any inability on his part, it's about having the right tools for the job.

The 12 Steps are your tools. Use them like a Magic 8 Ball, duct tape, or a Swiss Army knife. Dump any random problem you have through the steps like a strainer and see what you're left with. The steps don't solve any of my problems. What they do is help me see what my problems are, and in what order I need to solve them. I still have to figure out what to do, but the steps let me know where to start.

◇◇◇

The Crossing of the First Threshold. The hero must enter a new, strange land. There are all kinds of rules that don't apply back home. The hero may be lost and without a map.

Finding a recovery program is frightening at first. While you may be totally comfortable negotiating a drug deal or drinking in the scariest of bars, walking into a 12-Step group for the first time is scary. It's better to go with someone else, but plenty of people walk through that door alone for the first time.

◇◇◇

Rebirth: The Belly of the Whale. The hero appears to die, but she is actually reborn in another place. This takes place either literally or metaphorically. One way or another, the old self is dead, and the new self is ready to face the task ahead.

Admitting you're an alcoholic or addict is the first step. That's what makes you a recovering addict rather than an addict. You're not reborn a strong warrior, but you are moving categories. You're now ready for the next phase of adventure.

I also see the addict's life as similar to what Campbell refers to as "The Belly of the Whale." Often a hero is swallowed by a great beast. He's dead to the world. He can either emerge from the creature's belly or die where he is.

The addict in the same way creates a world around him that excludes his prior life. The only ones who know him anymore live in the same underworld he does. As far as his family goes, they often do not know his whereabouts.

Part Two: Initiation

The Road of Trials. The hero must face a series of small tasks or obstacles before the confrontation at the end of his quest. Sometimes this is merely finding his way. Other times, it is a series of smaller foes to be defeated before the "boss" character appears. This is the most standard way of developing the plot of a video game.

The Meeting with the Goddess. At some ridiculous location, like the top of the world or the bottom of the sea, the hero meets with the Goddess, who holds all knowledge of the cosmos. This is a vague part for me, as I'm not quite clear on its purpose. But as far as I can tell, she makes a man out of the hero with her seductive knowledge. Yep, she devirginates him. Again, maybe only metaphorically; as he's recently been reborn, this part takes him from being a boy to a man.

The correlation I draw here is in the fearless moral inventory that you have to draw up as part of your fourth step. You go deep into yourself, into the blackest parts of your mind, and find out who you really are and what you're doing here on Earth. In the fifth through seventh steps following, you transform internally; that is, you mature spiritually.

◇◇◇

Woman as Temptress. In many stories, the sexy woman is evil. The hero is led to her by her beauty, and she accepts him. But there is a condition that he discontinue his quest. Other times, she directly destroys him. The desires of the flesh get in the way of the journey's progress.

Don't read this only as men or women; this part is all about physical temptation. When drug use and drinking start, they feel really good. There are times that I remember a good high and I want to go out and get loaded. I feel the pull of the whiskey bottle into the store. But I know it will take me back to where I was. I can't have that one night of drinking without risking everything.

Dating sober is weird at first. I think the biggest urge to drink for me was on a first date. Every part of me wanted a shot or two to take the edge off. I didn't really know what to do on dates that didn't involve getting wasted.

Also, the women I was choosing were still the types I dated when I was a drunk. Often, they were drunks or drug addicts as well. The last thing you need while you're sobering up is your date getting wasted in front of you. For those of you with one alkie parent, you may not understand this. There are plenty of men and women out there who would love to go out on a date with someone who is sober. Trust me, awkward or shy is rated much better than loaded.

◇◇◇

Atonement with the Father. The father, for mythical purposes, is the authority figure in the story. While it may be a literal father, it's often a figurative father. The father figure may be a battle leader or a demanding god.

For me, this came in several parts. I had to give up my resentment against churches, schools, teachers, and my father, who had all exerted what I thought to be undue authority upon me. But the authority that I really had to embrace was the program itself.

I have so many negative approaches to recovery meetings. I don't like being in church buildings at all. I don't like people telling me what "God" can do for me. I don't like being told how I should live my life. But the meetings were the only place I could find the way to really heal myself. The point is, I need to not let my authority hang-ups stop me from getting the help I need.

◇◇◇

Apotheosis. The apotheosis is when a human crosses over into a divine entity. In some ancient cultures, a ruler achieved god status upon death, as decreed by the ruler's successor. In Campbell's hero theory, it's a knowledge-based deification, when the prophet goes from being just a person to an all-knowing and wise god-on-earth, worthy of worship.

You may hear the phrase "spiritual awakening" used in 12-Step circles. This is the moment they're talking about. It's a sudden gaining of knowledge so profound that it changes the individual's spirit permanently. It's the "Eureka!" "Aha!" "I get it!" moment of 12 Step. Honestly, most of 12 Step seemed like a real drag until, at some moment, I began to really enjoy it.

This was the moment when I became excited to be a part of the program. I applied its principles to every part of my life. I looked forward to my favorite meetings. I truly embraced its group nature.

◇◇◇

The Ultimate Boon. The hero is now ready to obtain that which he has set out to find, an item or new awareness that, once he returns with it, will benefit the society that he has left.

The hero has something that will help all his family or community back home. For instance, many stories tell about a single person finding or stealing fire and bringing it back to the tribe. It can also be knowledge.

The twelfth step is the one telling us all to carry the message to those who still suffer. Even though the eleven previous steps are the ones necessary for our immediate survival, it's not complete without bringing the message back. I've taken a number of old drinking buddies with me to meetings.

Part Three: Return

Refusal of the Return. After all the trials are completed, the hero doesn't always want to go back. He may not be seen as the hero in his old circles. His old land may not be as good as the new one. He is reluctant to share his knowledge with others.

Honestly, it's a pain in the ass to have sponsees and to keep commitments such as being the secretary at the meetings or even making the coffee. Suck it up. If it weren't for people doing these things, I wouldn't have gotten sober. Now it's my turn to help out.

◇◇

Honestly, it's a pain in the ass to have sponsees and to keep commitments such as being the secretary at the meetings or even making the coffee. Suck it up.

◇◇

◇◇◇

The Crossing of the Return Threshold. The hero returns to the "normal" world, which seems bizarre to him. After that long period of his life completing his task, the mundane life of normal humans makes no sense to him.

Going back into the Normie world after being a drunk or an addict for a long time takes awhile to adjust to. Most people have never used garbage bags to block out windows, nor have they smoked anything off tinfoil. They don't know the difference between speed and coke.

The Normies have their own system of living that must be learned, and they assume it's simple knowledge. Getting jobs, apartments, socializing, going on dates—all of these things seem foreign to someone living outside of it. You may know how to break up a pound of weed and sell it in eighth-ounce bags, but getting a job in an office is beyond you. What I did was ask people at meetings. You can ask them anything: how to do your laundry, how to find a dentist, how to work your stove. They will be relieved that other people did not know these things either.

◇◇◇

Master of Two Worlds. The hero is able to live in both the god realms and human realms. Maybe he comes back from the "dead."

This, to me, meant that at some point I could go out to nightclubs and bars without drinking. I really wanted to get back into performing, and most of the venues are in spots that sell liquor and give me free drink tickets. I got sober so I could live the life I wanted, not hide from it.

I also saw it as a return to the Normie world. I won't be a Normie again, but I can hang out with them again. When I first got sober, they made absolutely no sense to me. Although I'm mostly at home with recovering addicts, I can hang out with Normies without feeling socially awkward.

Recovery is where you find it. *Hero* spoke to me at a time when I needed inspiration. Maybe for you it will be a band, a movie, or a different piece of literature. *Hero* speaks of the human condition, as do many art forms. Keep your eyes open for answers in unlikely places.

Epilogue

Live Like
No One
Dares

People with a belief in an afterlife have a strong reason to get sober. Christians, for one, condemn gluttony as a sin that would keep them out of heaven. There's not a religion I know of that condones overindulgence. But what of the atheist or existentialist? Does it matter if you die sober or not? After all, we end up the same way, don't we?

It does matter how you live your life. I didn't always think so. I used to think that with 6 billion people in the world, individual action didn't affect humanity as a whole. But in a sense, you don't live with that many people in the world. Your world is made up of only a few hundred people, with a few thousand in your periphery. Your actual involved world is not very big, and you're a significant part of it.

Everyone gets a life. That's part of the deal. For some it may last only minutes, and for others it may last a hundred years. There are no guarantees on how long it is or how good it is. Maybe other people are right, and you get to come back again and again until you get it right, but we have no proof of that. What is true, no matter your religion or philosophy, is that we do get one at least. One life for everyone.

During fifteen years of drug and alcohol use, I talked about being a writer. I wrote one book in that whole time. Since then, this is my third book. I've also released a comedy CD. I was afraid I was giving up my writer's life to get sober, but just the opposite happened. I was able to achieve my goals, surprisingly easily, while sober.

I've done amazing things while sober. Since 2002, my life has been unreal. I've done shows on nights with musicians such as Fiona Apple and Joe Walsh. I've opened for heroes of mine like Jello Biafra and Lydia Lunch. I've gotten to know some really wonderful creative people like Greg Proops and Amber Tamblyn. I had an expense-paid trip to Australia.

Every day is a second chance for me. I could've easily died from drinking or from my drinking-induced chaos. I had a life and almost wasted it. I've had more fun since 2002 than I did the whole rest of my life. Every new person I meet, every new movie I see, every book I read are all things I would not have had had I not gotten my shit together.

Your best days are ahead of you. The movie starts when the guy gets sober and puts his life back together; it doesn't end there. Adventures await you. You can have whatever you want. Most of all, you can be happy.

My first year sober, I heard a guy share his story about going to Antarctica and living at a science facility there for a year. On a whim, he decided to go to Antarctica and got his affairs in order and did it. It struck me that I could go to Antarctica. I could go anywhere. I could do anything. But what did I want to do? I had no idea what I really wanted to do.

I spent the meeting stunned, realizing I could pursue any dream I had now that I wasn't being weighted down with this daily casting anchor of booze. I could go back to college. I could act in plays. I could film a movie. I could move anywhere in the country I wanted to go. There were infinite options, where months before the option was Get A Bottle Of Whiskey.

After the meeting, I found the speaker outside. I can't remember our conversation, I just remember what he said at the end of it: Be Great In Your Sobriety.

Wow, I thought, *I can be great! Now I have to figure out at what.* . . .

Just as most of this book is knowledge I have gained over late-night coffee, food, and milkshakes after meetings, this is my final message to pass on to you, as it was to me. It's time for you to get up and take what is yours. You matter. Be great in your sobriety.

ABOUT THE AUTHOR

Bucky Sinister is a recovering alcoholic who says about himself as a teen, "I took to alcohol immediately, a relationship that lasted fifteen years." Then he got help and got sober. He currently secretaries a meeting in San Francisco. He performs throughout the country at comedy and spoken word venues. He has published nine chapbooks and three full length collections of poetry, the most recent being *All Blacked Out & Nowhere to Go*. His first full-length CD, *What Happens in Narnia, Stays in Narnia* was released in 2007. He lives in San Francisco.

Visit him on the web at *www.buckysinister.com*.

To Our Readers

Conari Press, an imprint of Red Wheel/Weiser, publishes books on topics ranging from spirituality, personal growth, and relationships to women's issues, parenting, and social issues. Our mission is to publish quality books that will make a difference in people's lives—how we feel about ourselves and how we relate to one another. We value integrity, compassion, and receptivity, both in the books we publish and in the way we do business.

Our readers are our most important resource, and we value your input, suggestions, and ideas about what you would like to see published. Please feel free to contact us, to request our latest book catalog, or to be added to our mailing list.

Conari Press
An imprint of Red Wheel/Weiser, LLC
500 Third Street, Suite 230
San Francisco, CA 94107
www.redwheelweiser.com